General Knowledge 2020

Anand Pandey

SARK Publications
• Delhi • Patna

SARK Publications

• Delhi • Patna

Corporate Office: D-6,
Neel Kanth Apartment-2
Near HDFC Bank
Main Road, Sant Nagar
Burari, Delhi-110084

Mob. +91-8527227097 / 7701915858
Email: sarkpublications9@gmail.com

CONTENTS

ISBN : 97-8938611-7564
Price : ₹30

Typeset by: Chandan Kumar
9871773127

Printed & Bound By: Radha Offset, Delhi

WORLD & INDIAN GEOGRAPHY

WORLD GEOGRAPHY

UNIVERSE

- The study of universe is known as Cosmology.
- The universe is commonly defined as the totality of everything that exists including all physical matter and energy, the planets, starts, galaxies and the contents of intergalactic space.
- galaxy A galaxy is a vast system of billions of stars, dust and light gases bound by their own gravity. There are 100 billion galaxies in the universe and each galaxy has, on average, 100 billion stars.
- Our galaxy is Milky Way Galaxy (or the Akash Ganga) formed after the Big Bang.
- Andromeda is the nearest galaxy to the Milky Way.
- The Big Bang Theory Big Bang was an explosion of concentrated matter in the universe that occurred 15 billion years ago, leading to he formation of galaxies of stars and other heavenly bodies.
- It is believed that universe should be filled with radiation called the "cosmic microwave background." NASA has launched two mission to study these radiation, i.e. the Cosmic Background Explorer (COBE) and the Wilkinson Microwave Anistropy Probe (WMAP).
- Stars are heavenly bodies made up of hot burning gases and they shine by emitting their own light.
- Black Hole Stars heaving mass greater than three that of the Sun, have very high gravitational power, so that even light can not escape from its gravity and hence called black hole.
- Comets Made up of frozen gases. They move around the Sun in elongated elliptical orbit with the tail always pointing away from the Sun.
- Constellations The sky is divided into units to enable the astronomers to identify the position of the stars. These units are called constellations. There are 88 known constellations.
- Satellites are the heavenly bodies that revolve around the planets. Moon is the natural satellite of the Earth.

Facts about the Moon

Diameter	3476 km
Average distance from Earth	384365 km
Rotation Speed	27 days, 7 h, 43 min and 11.47 sec
Revolution Speed	27 days, 7 h, 43 min and 11.47 sec
Time taken by moonlight to reach the Earth	1.3 sec

Solar System

- The solar system consists of the Sun, eight planets and their satellites (or moons) and thousands of other smaller heavenly bodies such as asteroids, comets and meters.
- The Sun is at the centre of the solar system and all these bodies revolve around it. It is the nearest star to the Earth.

Facts about the sun

Average distance from the Earth	149598900 km
Diameter	1391980 km
Temperature of the Core	15000000°C
Rotation Speed	25.38 days (with respect to equator); 33 days (withe respect to poles)

Time taken by Sunlight to reach the Earth	8 min and 16.6 sec

Important Facts about

Biggest Planet	Jupiter
Biggest Satellite	Ganymede (Jupiter)
Blue Planet	Earth
Green Planet	Uranus
Brightest Planet	Vernus
Brightest Planet outside Solar System	Sirius (Dog Star)
Closest Star of Solar System	Proxima Centauri
Coldest Planet	Neptune
Evening Star	Venus
Farthest Planet from Sun	Neptune
Planet with maximum number of satellites	Jupiter
Fastest revolution in Solar System	Mercury
Hottest Planet	Venus
Densest Planet	Earth
Fastest rotation in Solar System	Jupiter
Morning Star	Venus
Nearest Planet to Earth	Venus
Nearest Planet to Sun	Mercury
Red Planet	Mars
Slowest Revolution in Solar System	Neptune
Slowest Rotation in Solar System	Venus
Smallest Planet	Mercury
Smallest Satellite	Deimos (Mars)
Earth' Twin	Venus
Only Satellite with an atmosphere like Earth	Titan

Asteroids (or Planetoids)

- Small planetary bodies that revolve around the Sun and found between the orbits of ars and Jupiter. Also known as minor planets.

Meteors and Meteorites

- Meteors are also called as shooting stars.
- meteors are fragments of rocks coming towards the Earth.
- They are formed due to collision among the asteroids.
- Meteorites are composed of various proportions of a nickel–iron alloy (10% nickel and 90% iron) and silicate minerals.
- Meteors that do not burn up completely in Earth's atmosphere and land on the Earth, are called meteorite.

Classification of Planets

Age	4550 million years
Mass	5.976 × 10 kg
Volume	1.083 10 kg
Mean Density	5.513 g/cm
Total Surface	510 million sq km
Land Area	29.2% of the total surface area
Water area	70.8% of the total surface area
Rotation Speed	23 hr. 56 min and 4.100 sec
Revolution Speed	365 days, 5 hr and 45.51 sec
Dates when days and nights are equal	March 21 (Vernal Equinox), 23rd September, (Autumnal Equinox)
Longest day	1st June, (summer Solstice) Sun is Vertically overhead to tropic of Cancer
Shortest night	22and December, (Winter Solstice) Sun is vertically overhead at Tropic of Capricorn
Escape Velocity	11.2 km/sec
Mean surface temperature	14°C

Major Mountains Peaks

Mountain Peak	Location

Mt Everest (Highest in the world)	Nepal-Tibet
K2 (Godwin Austin)	India (POK)
Dhaulagiri	Nepal
Annapurna	Nepal
Gurla Mandhata	Tibet
Tirich Mir	Pakistan
Aconcauga	Argentina
Cotopaxi	Ecuador
Kilimanjaro	Tanzania

Plateaus

Plateaus are flat, table like, upland areas with rough top surface and steep side walls.

Famous Plateaus of the World

Plateaus	Situation
Tibetan Plateau	Between Himalayas and Kunlun Mountains
Deccan Plateau	Southern India
Arabian Plateau	South-West Asia
Plateau of Brazil	Central-Eastern South America
Plateau of Mexico	Mexico
Plateau of Columbia	USA
Plateau of Madagascar	Madagascar
Plateau of Alaska	North-West North America
Plateaus of Bolivia	Andes Mountains
Great Basin Plateau	South of Columbia Plateau, USA
Colorado Plateau	South of Great Basin Plateau, USA

Plains

A relatively low-lying and flat land surface with least difference between its highest and lowest points in called a Plain.

Atmosphere

- The vast expanse of air,j which envelops the earth all around is called the atmosphere. It extends the thousands of kilometers.
- It protect the Earth's surface from the Sun's harmful ultraviolet rays.

Structure of Earth's Atmosphere

Layer	Height (km)	Feature
Troposphere	0-18 km	Contains 75% of the gases in the atmosphere. As height increase, temperature decreases (about 6.5° c/ km ascent).
Stratosphere	18-50 km	This layer contains the ozone layer. The temperature remains fairly constant. At upper layer temperature is almost 0°C.
Mesosphere	50-80 km	This is the coldest region of the atmosphere. the temperature drops to about-100°C
Ionosphere	80-600 km	Radio waves are bounced off the ions and reflect waves back to the Earth. This generally8 helps radio communication.
Exosphere	Above 600 km	Upper part of exosphere is called magnetosphere. The temperature keeps on rising constantly at high rate.

- The major constituents of air ion the atmosphere are Nitrogen (78%), Oxygen (21%), Argon (0.93%) and Carbon dioxide (0.03%).

- Besides water vapour, dust particles, smoke, salts and other impurities arc present in are in varying quantities.

Green House Effect and Global Warming

- A green house gas (sometimes abbreviated GHG) is a gas in the atmosphere that absorbs and emits radiation within the thermal infrared range. This process is the fundamental cause of the greenhouse effect.
- The primary greenhouse gases in the Earth's atmosphere are water vapour, carbon dioxide, methane, nitrous oxide and ozone.
- In the solar system, the atmosphere of Venus, Mars and Titan also contain gases that cause greenhouse effects.
- Global warming is the increase fo Earth's average surface temperature due to effect of greenhouse gases, such as carbon dioxide emissions from burning fossil fuels or from deforestation. This is a type of greenhouse effect.

Important Lakes of the World

Lake	Location
Caspian Sea	Asia
Superior	Canada and USA
Victoria	Africa
Huron	Canada and USA
Michigan	USA
Tanganyika	Africa
Baikal	Russia
Great Bear	Canada
Aral	Kazakhstan
Great Slave	Canada

Waterfalls

Waterfall	Locations
Angel Falls	Venezuela
Tugela Falls	South Africa
Monge	Norway
Yosemite	United States
Catarata Yumbilla	Peru

Riverside Cities

Town	River
Akyab (Myanmar)	Irrawaddy
Baghdad (Iraq)	Tigris
Basara (Iraq)	Tigris and Euphrates
Belgrade	Danube
Berlin (Germany)	Spree
Bristol (UK)	Avon
Budapest (Hungary)	Danube
Cairo (Egypt)	Nile
Canton	Si-Kiang
Glasgow (Scotland)	Clyde
Hamburg (Germany)	Elbe
Jamshedpur	Subarnarekha
Kabul	Kabul
Karachi	Indus
Khartoum (Sudan)	Nile
Lahore	Ravi
Lisbon (Portugal)	Tangus
London (UK)	Thames
Lucknow	Gomti
Montreal (Canada)	Ottawa
New Castle (UK)	Tyre
New Orleans (USA)	Mississippi
New York (USA)	Hudson
Paris (France)	Seine
Philadelphia (USA)	Delaware
Rome (Italy)	Tiber
Shanghai	Yang-tse-Kiang
Srinagar	Jhelum
Warsaw (Poland)	Vistula
Washington DC	Potomac
Yangon (Myanmar)	Irawady

Great deserts of the World

Name	Country/Region
Sahara (Libyan, Nubian)	North Africa
Australian (Gibson, Simpson),	Victorian
Great (Sandy)	Australia
Arabian (Rub al Khali, An-Nafud)	Arabia

Dasht-e-Lut (Barren Desert)	Iran
Desht-e-Kavir (Salt Desert)	Iran
Desierto de Sechura	Peru
Atacama	North Chile
Patagonia	Argentina
Kalahari	Botswana
Namib	Namibia

Minerals of the World

Mineral	Leading Producer
Gold	China
Bauxite	Australia
Copper	Chile
Platinum	South Africa
Chromium	South Africa
Vanadium	China
Antimony	China
Tungsten	China
Phosphate	Morocco
Manganese	China
Diamond	Russia
Iron ore	China
Petroleum	USA

Agriculture

Agricultural Produce	Leading Producer
Coffee	Brazil
Rubber	Thailand
Tea	China
Oil Palm	Indonesia
Cocoa	Ghana
Coconut	Indonesia
Date Palm	Egypt
Cotton	China
Wheat	China
Maize	USA
Fruits and Vegetables	China
Wool	Australia
Rice	China
Cloves	Zenzibar

Highest and Lowest Points of the Continent

Continent	Highest (m)	Lowest (m)
Asia	Mt Everest (8850)	Dead Sea (–396)
Asia	Mt Kilimanjaro (5895)	Lake Assal (–151)
North America	Mt McKinley (6190)	Death Valley (–87)
South America	Mt Aconcagua (6962)	Valdes Peninsula (–40)
Antarctica	Vinson Massif (4897)	Bentley Subglacial Trench (–2538)
Europe	Mt El' brus (5642)	Caspian Sea (–28)
Australia	Mt Kosciuszko (2280)	Lake Eyre (–16)

Important Industrial

Anshan (China)	Iron and Steel	Los Angeles (USA)	Petroleum
Baku (Azerbaijan)	Petroleum	Lyon (France)	Petroleum
Belfast (Ireland)	Iron and Steel	Magnitogorsk (Russia)	Silk Textiles

Birmingham (UK)	Petroleum	Manchester (UK)	Iron and Steel
Chicago (USA)	Ship-building	Milan (Italy)	Cotton Textile
Detroit (USA)	Iron and Steel	Multan (Pakistan)	Silk Textile
Havana (Cuba)	Cigars	Munich (Germany)	Pottery
Hollywood (USA)	Films	Nagoya (Japan)	Lenses
Johannesburg	Gold Mining	Philadelphia (USA)	Automobiles
Kansas City (USA)	Meat Packing	Pittsburgh (USA)	Locomotives
Kawasaki (Japan)	Iron and Stee	Plymouth (USA)	Iron and Steel
Kimberley (South Africa)	Diamond Mining	Rourkela (India)	Ship-building
Krivoi Rog (Ukraine)	Iron and Steel	Sheffield (UK)	Iron and Steel
Leeds (UK)	Woollen Textiles	Vladivostok (Russia)	Ship-building
Leningrad (Russia)	Ship-building	Wellington (New Zealand)	Dairy Products

INDIA GEOGRAPHY

India

- India is the seventh largest country in the world with an area of 3287263 sq km, which is 2.42% of world's area.
- India is the second most population country in the world with as population of 1.21 billion, which is 17.44% of the world.
- Indian subcontinent is located in the Northern and Eastern hemisphere.
- India shares longest boundary with Bangladesh (4096 km), followed by China (3488 km), Pakistan (3323 km), Nepal (1751 km), Myanmar (1643 km), Bhutan (699 km) and Afghanistan (106 km).
- In India, the Tropic of Cancer (23.5° N latitude) passes through 8 states (Gujarat, Rajasthan, Madhya Pradesh, Chhattisgarh, Jharkhand, West Bengal, Tripura and Mizoram.)
- Islands Andaman and Nicobar Islands on the Bay of Bengal; Lakshadweep, Amindive and Monicoy in the Arabian Sea.
- Ocean India lies midway between the Far East and Middle East. The trans-Indian Ocean routes connecting the industrially developed countries of Europe in the West and the under developed countries of East Asia close by Indian subcontinent if surrounded by Arabian Sea in the South-West and Bay of Bengal in the South-East.

Indian States Situated on the Border

Country	Border
Pakistan (4	Gujarat, Rajasthan, Punjab, Jammu and Kashmir
Afghanistan (1)	Jammu and Kashmir
China (5)	Jammu and Kashmir, Uttarakhand, Himachal Pradesh, Sikkim, Arunachal Pradesh
Nepal (5)	Uttar Pradesh, Uttrakhand, Bihar, West Bengal, Sikkim
Bhutan (4)	Sikkim, West Bengal, Assam, Arunachal Pradesh
Bangladesh (5)	West Bengal, Assam, Meghalaya, Tripura, Mizoram

Some of the Important Waterfalls of India

Waterfall	Height (km)	River	State
Kunchikal	455	Varahi	Karnataka
Jog/Gersoppa	260	Sharavati	Karnataka
Rakim Kund	168	Gaighat	Bihar
Chachai	127	Bihad	Madhya Pradesh
Kevti	98	Mahanadi	Madhya Pradesh
Sivasamudram	90	Gauveri	Karnataka

Important Lakes of India

Name of Lake	State	Important Fact
Chilka Lake	Odiash	It is a saline and lagoon lake (largest lake of India)
Colleru Lake	Andhra Pradesh	It is a freshwater lake.
Loktak Lake	Manipur	It is a freshwater lake having inland drainage in Manipur.
Lonar Lake	Maharashtra	It is a meteorite crater lake in Buldhana area of Maharashtra. The water is highly charged with Sodium carbonates and Sodium chloride.
Pangong Lake	Jammu and Kashmir	It is a salty lake.
Pulicat Lake	Tamil Nadu & Andhra Pradesh border	It is a saline and lagoon lake.
Sambhar Lake	Rajasthan	It is a shallow lake which is saline, located near Jaipur.
Tso Moriri Lake	Jammu and Kashmir	It is salty lake.
Vembanad Lake	Kerala	It is a lagoon lake.
Vular & Dal Lakes	Jammu and Kashmir	Wular lake was created due to tectonic activities.

Important Rivers of India

Name	Originates form	Falls into
Ganges	Combined Sources	Bay of Bengal
Sutlej	Mansarover Rakas Lakes	Chenab
Indus	Near Mansarover Lake	Arabian Sea
Ravi	Kullu Hills near Rothang Pass	Chenab
Beas	Near Rothang Pass	Sutlej
Jelum	Verinag in Kashmir	Chenab
Yanuna	Yamunotri	Ganga

Chamal	Singar Chouri Peak, Vindhyan escarpment	Yamuna
Ghaghara	Matsatung Glacier	Ganga
Kosi	Near Gosain Dham Peak	Ganga
Betwa	Vindhyanchal	Yamuna
Son	Amarkantak	Ganga
Brahmaputra	Near Mansarovar Lake	Bay of Bengal
Narmada	Amarkantak	Gulf of Khambat
Tapti	Betul District in Madhya Pradesh	Gulf of Khambat
Mahanadi	Raipur District in Chhattisgarh	Bey of Bengal
Luni	Aravallis	Rann of Kachchh
Ghaggar	Himalayas	Near Fatehabad
Sabarmati	Mewar hill, Aravallis	Gulf of Khambat
Krishna	Western Ghats	Bey of Bengal
Godavari	Nasik district in Maharashtra	Bey of Bengal
Cauveri	Brahmagir Range of Western Ghats	Bey of Bengal
Tungabhadra	Western Ghats	Krishna

AGRICULTURE

India is essentially an agricultural land. Two-thirds of its population still lives on agriculture. It includes farming, animal rearing and fishing.

Agricultural Seasons in India

There are there major crop seasons in India.

Kharif

Sown in June/July, harvested in September/October, e.g., rice, jowar, bajra, ragi, maiza, cotton and jute.

Rabi

Sown in October/December, harvested in April/May e.g., wheat, barley, peas, rapeseed, mustard, grains.

Zaid

Sown in February/March harvested in May/June, e.g., urad, moong, melons etc.

Green Revolution

It is the phrase generally used to describe the spectacular increase that took place during 1968 and is continuing in the production of foodgrains in India.

The Components of Green Revolution are

High Yield Variety Seeds, Irrigation, use of Fertilis2ers, Use of Insecticide and Pesticide, Command Area Development, Programme Consolidation of Holdings etc.

Chief Crops and Producing States

Type	Name	Major Producers
Cereals	Wheat	Uttar Pradesh, Punjab and Madhya Pradesh
	Rice	West Bengal and Uttr Pradesh

	Gram	Madhya Pradesh and Tamil Nadu
	Barley	Maharashtra, Uttar Pradesh and Rajasthan
	Bajra	Maharashtra, Gujarat and Rajasthan
Cash Crops	Sugarcane	Uttar Pradesh and Maharashtra
	Poppy	Uttar Pradesh and Himachal Pradesh
Oil Seeds	Coconut	Kerala and Tamil Nadu
	Linseed	Rajasthan, Madhya Pradesh and Haryana
	Groundnut	Gujarat, Andhra Pradesh and Tamil Nadu
	Rape seed and mustard	Rajasthan, Madhya Pradesh and Haryana
	Sesame	Uttar Pradesh and Rajasthan
	Sunflower	Karnataka, Andhra Pradesh and Maharashtra
Fiber Crops	Cotton	Maharashtra and Gujarat
	Jute	West Bengal and Bihar
	Silk	Karnataka and Kerala
	Hemp	Madhya Pradesh and Uttar Pradesh
Plantations	Coffee	Karnataka and Kerala
	Rubber	Kerala and karnataka
	Tea	Assam and Kerala
	Tobacco	Gujarat, Maharashtra and Madhya Pradesh
Spices	Pepper	Kerala, Karnataka and Tamil Nadu
	Cashewnuts	Kerala, Tamil Nadu and Andhra Pradesh
	Ginger	Kerala and Uttar Pradesh
	Turmeric	Andhra Pradesh and Odisha

MINERAL RESOURCES

Types of Minerals

Metallic Iron ore, copper, aluminium, tin, lead, gold and silver.
Non-metallic Coal, mica, manganese, petroleum and sulphur.
Radioactive Uranium and thorium

Mineral Resources of India

Mineral	States
Coal	West Bengal, Jharkhand, Odisha, Madhya Pradesh and Chhattisgarh
Copper	Madhya Pradesh, Rajasthan, Jharkhand, Karnataka
Gold	Karnataka, Andhra Pradesh
Iron	Karnataka, Chhattisgarh and Jharkhand
Bauxite	Odisha, Jharkhand, Gujarat and Madhya Pradesh
Mica	Jharkhand, Andhra Pradesh and Rajasthan
Petroleum	Assam, Gujarat, Mumbai High, Bassein (South of Mumbai High)
Uranium	Jharkhand, Rajasthan, Andhra Pradesh and Karnataka
Thorium	Kerala Coast, Rocks and Aravalli in Rajasthan

Silver, Zinc and Lead	Rajasthan, Andhra Pradesh, Karnataka (Kolar mines)
Diamong	Panna (Madhya Predesh), Banda (Uttar Pradsh)

TRANSPORTATION IN INDIA

Railways

Indian Railway system in the second largest Asia and the fourth largest in the world.

- The Indian Railways operate in three different gauges.
  Board Gauge
  (Distance between rails in 1.676 m)
  Metre Gauge
  (Distance between rails is 1.00 m)
  Narrow Gauge
  (Distance between rails is 0.762 or 0.610)
- The longest railway platform in India is now Gorakhpur with a stretch of around 1.3 km.

Railway Zone	Headquarters
Central	Mumbai
Eastern	Kolkata
Northern	New Delhi
North-Eastern	Gorakhpur
North-Eastern Frontier	Maligaon-Guwahati
Southern	Chennai
South-Eastern	Secunderabad
Western	Kolkata
East Coast	M nbai Ch rchgate
East Central	Bhubaneshwar
North Central	Hajipur
North-Western	Allahabad
South-Western	Jaipur
West Central	Hubli
South-East Central	Jaipur
Kolkata Metro	Kolkata

- The first train ran in India between Bombay and Thane, a stretch of 34 km on 16th April, 1853.
- The second train run between Howrah and Hooghly.
- The first electric train in India was Deccan Queen. It was introduced in 1929 between Bombay and Poona.
- The longest train route is 'Vivek Express' from Dibrugarh in Assam to Kanyakumari in Tamil Nadu. It covers a distance of 4273 km (2655 miles).
- The first Metro train was introduced in Kolkata (West Bengal) on 24th October, 1984. The two stations connected were Dumdum and Belgachhila.
- Indian railways has a network of 7030 stations spread over a route length of 63974 km with a fleet of 8593 locomotives.
- Delhi metro rail was approved in 1996 but is was started in 2002 on 25th December between Shahdra and Tess Hazari.
- Rapid metro train has been started in Gurgaon (Harayana) on November 14, 2013.
- Road Transport
- India has one of the largest road network in the world (48 lakh km approx). It consists of National highways, State highways; major/other district roads and rural roads.
- NH 44 (3745 km) is the longest highway of India.
- NH 47A is the smallest highway of India.
- NS-EW Corridor intersect at Jhansi.
- Maharashtra has the maximum length of surfaced roads in India.

Important National Highways

NH	Connects
NH 1	New Delhi-Ambala-Jalandhar-Amritsar
NH 2	Delhi-Mathura-Agra-Kanpur-Allahabad-Varanasi-Kolkata
NH 3	Agra-Gwalior-Naskik-Mumbai

NH 4	Thane and Chennai via Pune and Bengalure
NH 5	Kolkata-Chennai
NH 6	Kolkata-Dhule
NH 7	Varanasi-Kanyakumari (2369 km)
NH 8	Delhi-Mumbai (via Jaipur, Vadodra and Ahmedabd)
NH 9	Mumbai-Vijaywada
NH 10	Delhi-Fazika
NH 24	Delhi-Lucknow
NH 26	Jhansi-Lakhnadon

Air Transport

- JRD Tata was the first person to take a solo flight from Mumbai to Karachi in 1931.
- In 1935, the 'Tata Air Lines' started its operation between Mumbai and Thiruvananthapuram and in 1937 between Mumbai and Delhi.
- In 1953, all the private airline companies were nationalised and Indian Airlines and Air India came into existence.
- Vayudoot Limited started in 1981 as a private air carrier and later on it merged with India Airlines.
- International Airport Authority of India and National Airports Authority were merged on 1995 to form Airports Authority of India.
- The Authority manages the Civil Aviation Training College at Allahabad and National Institute of Aviation Management and Research at Delhi.

Major International Airports in India

Rajiv Gandhi International Airport	Hyderabad
Calicaut International Airport	Calicut
Chhatrapati Shivaji International Airport	Mumbai
Kempe gowda International Airport	Bengaluru
Goa Airport in Vasco di Gama City	Goa
Lokpriya Gopinath Bordoloi International Airport	Guwahati
Sardar Vallabhbhai Patel International Airport	Ahmedabad
Indira Gandhi International Airport	Delhi
Chennai International Airport	Chennai
Shri Guru Ram Dass Jee International Aiport	Amritsar

ENVIRONMENT AND ECOLOGY

- Environment All external conditions, factors, matter and energy living and non-living that affect any living organism or other specified system.
- Ecology Biological science that studies the relationships between living orgnaisms and their environment; study of the structure and factions of nature.
- Ecosystem It is defined as a unit which include all the organisms (biological components) in a given are interacting with the environment (physical component), so that the flow energy leads to a clearly defined trophic structure, biotic diversity8 and material cycles.
- Biome Terrestrial regions charecterised by certain types of vegetation and other forms of life. Examples include various types of deserts, grasslands and forests.
- Wetland Land that is covered all part of the time with saltwater or freshwater, excluding streams, lakes and the open ocean.
- Biodiversity Veriety of different species (species diversity), genetic variability among individuals within each species (genetic diversity), variety fo ecosystems (ecological diversity) and functions such as energy flow and matter cycling needed for the survival of species and biological communities (functional diversity).
- Biosphere Zone of the Earth where life is found. It consists fo part of

the atmosphere (the troposphere) hydrosphere (mostly surface water and groundwater) and lithosphere (mostly soil and surface rocks and sediments on the bottoms of oceans and other bodies of water) where life is found. Compare atmosphere, geosphere, hydrosphere.

- Wildlife All free, undomesticated species. Sometimes the term is used to describe animals only.
- Threatened Species Wild species that is still abundant in is natural rages but is likely to become endangered because of decline in numbers.
- Ozone (O) Colourless and highly reactive gas and a major component of photochemical smog. Also found in the ozone layer in the stratosphere and protect us from ultra violet rays.
- Smog Originally, a combination of smoke and fog but now used to describe other mixture of pollutants in the atmosphere.
- Acid Rain It refers to the precipitation with elevated levels of hydrogen ions or al low pH. When fossil fuel is burnt, oxides are formed in the atmosphere. The oxides formed are carbon oxides, sulphur oxides and nitrogen oxides. All of these oxides form the acidic solution when they dissolve in water.
- Global Warming Warming of the Earth's lower atmosphere (troposphere) because of increases in the concentrations of one or more greenhouse gases. It c n result in irreversible climate change that can last for decades to thousands of years.
- Coral Bleaching Coral bleaching occurs when the relations between the coral host and zooxanthallae, which give coral much of their colour, breaks down. Without the zooxanthallae, the tissue of the coral animal appears transparent and the coral's bright white skelton reveald.
- Sustainability Ability of Earth's various systems, including human cultural systems and economies, to survive and adapt to changing environmental conditions indefinitely.

Environment related Important International Agreement/Conference

Un conference on the Human Environment	Stockholm (1972)
Convention on Migratory Species	Bonn (1979)
Convention for the Protection of the Ozone Layer	Vienna (1985)
Pototocol on Substances that Deplete the Ozone Layer	Montreal (1987)
Convention on the Transboundary Movement of Hazardous Wastes	Basel (1989)
East Summit (Un Conference on Environment and Development)	Rio-de-Janeiro (1992)
Convention on Prior Informed Consent	Rotterdam (1998)
Un Conference of Sustainable Development	Rio-de-Janeiro (2012)
Nagoya Protocol on Genetic Resources (Nagoya Protocol)	Nagoya (2010)
Convention on biological Diversity (CBD-CoP-11)	Hyderabad (2012)
Lima Climate Change Conference (CoP-20)	Lima (2014)
Paris agreement (Cop-21)	Paris (2015)
Marrakech Conference (Cop-22)	Marrakech Morocco (2016)

Wildlife Conservation in India

Project	Year
Project Hangul	1970
Project Gir	1972
Project Tiger	1973
Project Olive Riddey Turtles	1975
Crocodile Breeding Scheme	1975
Project Manipur Thamin	1977
Project Rhino	1987
Project Elephant	1992
Project Red Panda	1996
Project Vulture	2006

Endangered Species in India

Birds	Great Indian Bustard, Forest Owlet, Valture, Himalayan Quail, Siberian Crane
Mammals	Flying Squirrel, Red Panda, Pygmy Hog, Kondana Rat, Snow Leopard, Asiatic Loin, One-Horned Rhinoceros
Reptiles	Gharial, Hawksbill Turtle, River Terrapin, Sispara Day Gecko
Amphibians	Flying Frog, Tiger Toad

INDIAN POLITY

CONSTITUTION

Framing of the Indian Constitution

- The idea to have a constitution was given by MN Roy (A pioneer of Communist Movement of India).
- The Constitutions was framed by the Constituent Assembly of India, set-up on May 16, 1946, in accordance with the Cabinet Mission Plan, under the Chairmanship of Sachchinand Sinha, initially. Dr Rajendra Prasad and HC Mukherjee were elected as the President and Vice-President respectively on 11th December 1945. BN Rau was appointed as the Constitutional Advisor.
- The total membership of the Constituent Assembly was 389 of these 292 were representatives of British States; 93 were representatives of Princely States and 4 were from the chief Commissioners Provinces of Delhi, Ajmer-Marware, Coorg and British Baluchistan,
- The Chairman of the Drafting Committee was Dr BR Ambedkar, also known as the father of the Indian Constitution.
- Dr BR Ambedkar was elected from Bengal for constitutional Assembly.

Enactment of the Constitution

- The Constituent Assembly took 2 years, 11 months and 18 days to complete the Constitution.
- Some of the provision related to citizenship, elections, provisional Parliament etc were given immediate effect.
- The Constitution, was adopted on November 26, 1949, contained a Preamble 395 Articles divided into 22 Parts and 8 Schedules. Presently, it has 465 Articles divided into 25 Parts and 12 Schedules.
- The Constitution was delayed till January 26, 1950 because, in 1930 on this day Indian National Congress demanded Poorna Swaraj in Lahore Session, Chaired by JL Nehru.
- The Constitution came into force on 26th January, 1950, known as Republic Day of Indian. The Constituent Assembly adopted out National Flag on July 26, 1947. It was designed by Pingali Venkayya.

Interim Government (1946)

Member	Portfolios Held
Jawaharlal Nahru	External Affairs & Commonwealth Relations
Sardar Vallabbhai Patel	Home, Information & Broadcasting
Dr Rajendra Prasad	Food & Agriculture
Dr John Mathai	Industries & Supplies
Jagivan Ram	Labour
Sardar Baldev Singh	Defence
CH Bhabha	Works, Mines & Power
Liaquat Ali Khan	Finance
Abdur REab Nishtar	Posts & Air
Asaf Ali	Railways & Transport
C Rajagopalachari	Education & Arts
II Chundrigar	Commerce
Ghaznafar Ali Khan	Health
Joginder Nath Mandal	Law

- The members of the interim government were members of the Viceroy's Executive Council. The Viceroy continued to be the head of the Council.
- Jawaharlal Nehru was designated as the Vice- President of the Council.

Preamble

- It is the preface or the introduction of the Constitution. It is an integral part of the Constitution. The interpretation of the Constitution is based on the3 spirit of the Preamble.
- The Objective Resolution was drafted and moved by Jawaharlal Nehru and adopted by the Constituent Assembly, ultimately became the Preamble.
- The language of the Preamble was borrowed from the Constitution of USA.
- The words, Socialist, Secular and integrity were added by the 42nd Constitutional Amendment Act-1976.

The Preamble

"WE, THE PEOPLE OF INDIA, having solemnly resolved to constitute India into a SOVERIGN, SOCIALIST, SECULAR, DEMOCRATIC REPUBLIC and to secure to tall its citizens.
JUSTICE, Social, Economic and Political
LIBERTY of though, expression, belief, faith and worship;
EQUALITY of status and of opportunity; and to promote among them all
PRATERNITY assuring the dignity of the individual and the unity and integrity of the Nation; IN OUR CONSTITUENT ASSEMBLY this twenty-sixth day of November, 1949 do HEREBY ADOPT, ENACT AND GIVE TO OURSELVES THIS CONSTITUTION.

Sources of the Indian Constitution

UK	Rule of Law
	Cabinet Writs
	Prerogative Writs
	Bicameral Parliament
	CAG Office
	Single Citizenship
	Law making procedures
USA	Written Constitution
	Vice-President as the Ex-officio Chairman of Upper House
	Fundamental Rights
	Supreme Court
	Provision of States
	Independence of Judiciary and Judicial Review
	Preamble
USSR	Fundamental Duties
Australia	Concurrent List
	Joint sitting in the Preamble
	Joint sitting in the Preamble
Japan	Procedure established by law
Germany	Suspension of Fundamental Rights during the Emergency
Canada	Scheme of federation with a strong Centre
	Distribution of powers between the Centre and the States and placing Residuary Powers with the Centre
Ireland	Concept of Directive Principles of State Policy method of election of the President
South Africa	Procedure for amendment of the constitution and election of member of Rajya Sabha
France	Republic and the ideals of Liberty equality and fraternity in the Preamble

Main Features

- Combination of Rigidity and Flexibility
- Bulkiest written Constitutions in the World.
- Parliamentary System of Government
- federal System with a Unitary bias
- Fundamental Rights and Duties
- Directive Principles of State Policy
- Universal Adult Franchise
- Integrated and Independent Judiciary Single citizenship
- Emergency Powers

IMPORTANT ARTICLES

Part I

Union and its Territories (Article 1-4)

1. The Constitution says, "India, that is Bharat, shall be a Union of States".
2. Admission or establishment of new States.
3. The Constitutions empowers the Parliament to form new States and to alter the areas, boundaries or names of existing States.

- Jammu and Kashmir has been given special status under Article 370.

Part II

Citizenship (Article 5-11)

The Citizenship Actg of 1955 prescribes five ways to acquire citizenship of India

1. By birth
2. By descent
3. By registration
4. By naturalisation
5. By incorporation

Three modes of losing citizenship

1. Renunciation
2. Termination
3. Deprivation

Part III

Fundamental Rights (Article 12-35)

Rights to Equality (Article 14-18)

- Equality before Law (Article 14)
- Prohibition of discrimination on ground of religion, race, caste, sex or place of birth (Article 15)
- Equality of opportunity in matters of public employment. (Article 16)
- Abolition of untouchablity (Article 17)
- Abolition of titles. (Article 18)

Rights to Freedom (Article 19-22)

- Protection of certain rights regarding; Speech and expression, assembly, association, movement, residence, and profession (Article 19)
- Protection in respect of conviction for of fences (Article 20)
- Protection of life and personal liberty (Article 21)
- Protection against arrest and detention in certain cases (Article 22).

Right to Education

- Article 21A states that the state shall provide free and compulsory education to all children of the age of 6-14 years.

Rights against Exploitation (Article 23-24)

- Prohibition of human trafficking and forced labour (Article 23.)
- Prohibition of employment of children in any factories, etc. (Article 24)
- Freedom of Press is implicit in the Article 19, and Article 20 and 21 cannot be suspended under Article 352 (National Emergency)
- Right to Property Article 19(1)(f) was repealed by the 44th Amendment Act, 1978, and was made a legal right under Article 300A.

Rights to Freedom of Religion (Article 25-28)

- Freedom of conscience and right to profess, practice and propagate one's religious beliefs.
- Freedom to manage religious affairs (Article 26)
- Freedom from taxation for promotion of any particular religion (Article 27).
- Freedom from attendance of religious instructions or religious worship in certain educational institutions (Article 28).

Cultural and Educational Rights

- Protection of interest of minorities (Article 29)
- Rights of minorities to establish and administer educational institutions (Article 30)

Rights to Constitutional Remedies

- Right to move to the Supreme Court (Article 32) and the High Courts (Article 226) in case of violation of the Fundamental Rights BR Ambedkar called Article 32 as the Heart and Soul of the Constitution.
- Writs of hebeas ocrpus, mandamus, prohibition, certiorari and quo-warranto can be issued for this.

Part IV

Directive Principles of State Policy (Article 36-51)

Directive principles are broad guiding principles that states shall keep in mind while formulating policies and enacting laws. These are non–justiciable in nature.

Article 36-37 Definition and application of the principles contained in this part.

Article 38 To secure and protect a social order, which stands for the welfare of the people.

- Article 39 Certain principles of policy to be followed by the State.
- Article 40 To organise village Panchayats as units of self-government.
- Article 41 Right to work, to education and to public assistance in certain cases.
- Article 42 To secure just and humane conditions of work and maternity relief.
- Article 43 Living wage etc for workers, To promote cottage industries.
- Article 44 Uniform Civil Code for the citizens.
- Article 45 Provision of early childhood care and education to children below the age of 6 years.
- Article 47 Improvement of public health and the prohibition of intoxicating drinks and drugs.
- Article 48 Organisation fo agriculture an animal husbandry on modern lines.
- Article 49 To protect all monuments of historic interest and national importance.
- Article 50 To bring about the separation of the judiciary from the executive.
- Article 51 Promotion of international peace and security.

Part IV (A)

Fundamental Duties (Article 51A)

It was inserted by the 42nd Amendment Act 1976 on the recommendations of Swaran Singh Committee it was inspired by the Constitution of USSR (Now Russia).

It shall be the duty of every citizen of India

- to abide by the Constitution and respect its idedals and institutions, the National Flag and the National Anthem.
- to cherish and follow the noble ideals which inspired our national struggle for freedom.
- 3. to uphold and protech the sovereignty, unity and integrity of India.
- to defend the country and render national service, when called up to do so.
- to promote harmony and the spirit of common brotherhood amongst all the people of India. transcending religious, linguistic and regional or sectional diversitics; to renounce practices derogatory to the dignity of women.
- to value and preserve the rich heritage of our composite culture.
- to protech and imprové the natural environment including forests, lakes, rivers and wildlife and to have compassion for living creatures.
- to devlop scientific temper, humanism and the spirit of enquiry and reform.
- to safeguard public property and to abjure violence.
- to strive towards excellence in all spheres of individula and collective activity, so that the nation constantly rises to higher levels of endeavour and achievement.
- Each opportunities for education to his child or ward between the age of 6 and 14 years.
- Last fundamental Duty was inserted by 86th Constitutional Amendment Act 2002.

Part V

Union (Article 52-151)

The president

- Executive Head of the State and the first citizen of India.
- The 42nd Constitution Amendment 1976 of has made it obligatory on he

part of the President to accept the advice of the Coucil of Ministers. However, 44th Amendent Act amended the word 'obligatory' and added that 'President can send the advice for reconsideration'.

- **Qualifications** Must be citizen of India; of 35 years in age; eligible ot be a member of the Lok Sabha and must not hold any office of profit.
- **Election** Indirectly elected thorugh Electoral college consisting of elected members of both the Houses of the Parliament and elected members of the Legislative Assemblies of the States and elected members of the Legislative Assemblies of Union Territories of Delhi and Puducherry.
- Members of the Legislative Councils have no right to vote in the Presidential election.
- Supreme Court decides all disputes regarding President's election.
- **Tenure** The term is 5 years though there is no upper limit on the number of times a person can become the President (Article 57). He can give resignation to the Vice–President before the full-term.
- The salary of the President is 150000 per month.
- Incase, the office of the President falls vacant due to death, resignation or removal, the Vice-President acts as the President.
- If he is not available then Chief Justice of India, if not then the senor most Judge of the Supreme Court shall act as the President of India.
- The first and only President who dies in the office, was Dr Zakir Hussain. he was also the President withe the shortest tenure.
- Justice M Hidayatullah was the first Chief Justice of India to be appointed as the President (July 1969-August 1969).

Impeachment Procedure

- It is a quasi-judicial procedure, President ca be impeached only on the grounds of violation of the Constitution. (Article 61)
- The impeachment procedure can be initiated in either House of the Parliament.

Powers of President

- He is the formal head of the administration.
- The President shall have the power to appoint and remove high authorities like the Prime Minister other Ministers of the Union, Judges, Governors of States and appoints Chiefs of Army, Navy and Air Force.
- He nominates 12 members of the Rajya Sabha from persons of literature. art, science and social work and 2 members in the Lok Sabha of the Anglo–Indian Community.
- Declares wars and concludes peace, subject to the approval of the Parliament.
- President has the Veto power.
- Under Article. 72, the President has the power to grant pardons, reprieves, respites or remission of punishment or to suspend, remit or commute the sentence of any person convicted with death sentence.
- Under Article 123, President can promulgate Ordinances, when the Parliament is not in session.

Types of Vetoes

- Absolute Veto Withholding the assent to the Bill.
- Qualified Veto Can be overridden by the legislature with a higher majority.
- Suspensive Veto Can be overridden by the Legislature with an ordinary majority.
- Pocket Veto in giving assent to the Bill. The Veto Power has been exercised only twice (a) by Dr Rajendra Prasad and (b) by R. Venkata raman. The above four the President of India is vested with three vetos absolute veto, suspensive veto and pocket veto, There is no qualified veto in the case of Indian President.

Emergency Powers

- To declare National Emergency (Article 352)
- To impose President Rule in a State. (Article 356 and 365)
- To declare Financial Emergency (Article 360)

Vice-President

- Article 63 of the Constitution stipulates a Vice-President for India.

- he is elected by both the House of Parliament.
- The Vice-President is the Ex-officio Chairman of the Council of States (Rajya Sabha) as mentioned in the Article 64
- Present salary of the Vice–President is per month.
- The first Vice-President of India was Dr S Radhakrishnan.
- The first and only Vice-President who died in the office, was Shri Krishna Kant (1997-2002).

Council of Ministers

- Article 74 of the Constitution states that there shall be a Council of Ministers, with the Prime Minister at its head, to aid and advise the President.
- It is composed of all Union Minister— the Prime Minister, Cabinet Ministers, Ministers of State (Indepent) and Minister of State.
- The other Ministers shall be appointed by the President on the advice of the Prime Minister under Article 75(1)
- A Minister must be a member of either House of Parliament or be elected within 6 months of assuming office under Article 75(5).
- The Council of Ministers is collectively responsible to the Lok Sabha, that is,a vote of no confidence even against a single Minister means that entire Council must resign [Article 75 (3)].
- Ministers are also responsible for their departments and can be removed from the office by the President on the advice of the Prime Minister. This is essentially an individual responsibility under Article 75 (2).

Prime Ministers

- The Prime Minister is the head of the Government and the head of the Council of Ministers.
- The Prime Minister is appointed by the President on the basis of this being the leader of the majority party in the Lok Sabha.
- If no party gets an absolute majority in the Lok Sabha or a Prime Minister resigns or dies, the President can use his own discretion in the choice of the Prime Minister.
- Article 78 stipulates that is is the duty of the Prime Minister (a) to communicate to the President all the decisions taken by the Cabinet and (b) to furnish such information relating to the administration of the Union or any Legislaton as the President may call for. The Prime Minister serves in the office for five years through he can be re–appointed.
- When the Lok Sabha is dissolved, He can continue in office upon the request of the President.
- If the Government is defeated in the Lok Sabha, the Prime Minister and the entire cabinet must resign, however, if defeated in the Rajya Sabha[resignation is not obligatory.

Facts

- Jawaharlal Nehru was the first Prime Minister and the longest serving so far.
- The first and the 'only' acting Prime Minister was Gulzarilal Nanda.
- Lal bahadur Shastri was the first PM who died abroad, while in office at Takshent, Gulzarilal Nanda has acted twice as the Interim Prime Minister.
- Chaudhary Charan Singh was the only PM who did not face Parliament, while being in office.
- The youngest Prime Minister was Rajeev Ghandi and the oldest Prime Minister was Morarji Desai.
- AB Vajpayee (May 1996-June 1996) government had the shortest tenure (13 days).

Union Legislature

- Legislature of the Union is called the Parliament and consists of the Rajya Sabha (Council of States), the Lok Sabha (House of the People) and the President (Article 79).
- The business of Parliament is transacted either in Hindi or in English. However, the Presiding Officers of the two Houses may permit any member to address the House in his/her mother tongue too.

Rajya Sabha (Council of States)

- Rajya Sabha is the Upper House of the Parliament and the first sitting of the Rajya Sabha was held on April 3,1952.
- The maximum permissible strength of

the Rajya Sabha is 250. Of these, 238 members are elected indirectly from the States and Union Territories, and 12 are nominated by the President for their expertise in art, literature, science and social service (Article 80).

- Currently, the strength of the Rajya Sabha is 245. Of these, 229 members are elected from states and 4 members represent Union Territories and 12 members are nominated by the President.
- The Rajya Sabha is a Permanent House and is not subject to dissolution and members enjoy its a tenure of six years. However, one-third of the members retire every second years (Article 83).
- It shares legislative power with the Lok Sabha, except in the case of Money Bill where the Lok Sabha has overriding powers.

Lok Sabha (People's House)

- The Lok Sabha is the Lower House of the Parliament and its first sitting took place on May 13, 1952. The current Lok Sabha is the 16th constituted Lok Sabha.
- Three Sessions of the Lok Sabha are held every year, namely Budget Session (February to May); Monsoon Session (July to September); and winter Session (November to December).
- Members 530 from States 20 from Union Territories and 2 nominated by the President, from the Anglo Indian Community.
- Election The representatives of the states are directly elected by the people of the state on the basis of adult suffrage.
- **Qualification** for Members of the Parliament Article 84 provides for the eligibility for membership of the Parliament. The conditions are
  - (a) citizen of India.
  - (b) at least 25 years of age for the Lok Sabha and 30 years of age for the Rajya Sabha; and
  - (c) posses such other qualifications as may be prescribed by the Parliament.
- Bills It may be classified as Ordinary, Money, Financial and Constitutional Amendments.
- The Ordinary Bills ca be introduced in either House of the Parliament, but Money Bill can be initiated only in the House of the People. (Article 110)
- After a Money Bill has been passed by the Lok Sabha, it is sent to the Rajya Sabha for deliberation. The Rajya Sabha is given 14 days to make recommendations, which can be accepted or not by the Lok Sabha.
- Article 111 stipulates that a Money Bill cannot be returned to the House by the President for reconsideration.

Speaker of the Lok Sabha

- As soon as a new Lok Sabha is constituted, the President appoints a Speaker pro-tem, who is generally the senior most member of the House.
- Speaker is the head of Lok Sabha. He/She is elected from amongst the members of Lok Sabha. The Speaker of the Lok Sabha conducts the business in the House. A Deputy Speaker is also elected to officiate in the absence of the Speaker.

Facts

- GV Mavalnkar was the first Speaker of the Lok Sabha (1952-1956).
- MA Ayyangar was the first Deputy Speaker (1952-1956).
- Dr Balram Jakhar was the longest serving Speaker (1980-1989).
- GMC Balyogi is the first Speaker to die in the office (1998-2002).
- Meria Kumar is the first woman speaker of the Lok Sabha (2009-2013).
- Sumitra Mahajan (2014-Present).

Supreme Court

The supreme Court of India was inaugurated on January 28, 1950. Presently, there are 23 sitting judges in Supreme Court against a sanctioned strength of 31 including chief justice of India. A small Bench, with two to three Justices, is called a Division Bench. A large Bench, with five or more Justices, is called a Constitutional Bench.

Tenure and Qualification

- Judges of the Supreme Court are appointed by the President and retire at the age of 65.

- The qualifications are (a) must be a citizen of India; (b) a Judge of High Court for at least 5 years; or (c) an advocate of a High Court for at least 10 years; or he should be a distinguished jurist in the opinion of the President.
- The Constitution has not prescribed a minimum age for appointment as a judge of the Supreme Court.
- **Independence of Judges** (Article 125) The salaries and allowances of Judges are charged from the Consolidated Fund of India (Present salary fo the CJI is and of other Judges is).
- **Removal of Judges** Judges can be removed only on the grounds of proved misbehaviour or incapacity.
- Judges can be removed only by a resolution of both Houses of Parliament supported by a majority of total membership of both the Houses and 2/3 of members present and voting. The first Judge against whom the proceedings were initiated was **V Ramaswami** (1993) and the second one was Sumitra Sen (2011).
- CR Karnan is first judge who was punished

Jurisdiction

The Supreme Court has original, appellate, advisory and write jurisdictions.

- Original Jurisdiction means that certain types of cases can originate with the Supreme Court only. The Supreme Court has original jurisdiction in (a) disputes between the centre and one or more States; (b) disputes between the Centre and any State(s) on one side and one or more States on the other side; (c) disputes between two or more States; and (d) disputes regarding the enforcement of Fundamental Rights.
- Appellate Jurisdiction means that appeals against judgements of lower courts can be referred to it. the Supreme Court is the highest court of appeal in the country. Four types of cases fall within its appellate jurisdiction, namely, constitutional cases, civil cases, criminal cases and appeals by special leave.

Facts

- The first Chief Justice of India was HJ Kania (1950-51).
- The shortest tenure so far is of KN Singh (November 25, 1991-December 12, 1991).
- The longest tenure, so far is of YV Chandrachud (1978-85).
- The first woman Judge of the Supreme Court was Justice Fatima Beevi in 1987 and the second woman Justice was Gyan Sudha Mishra in 2010.
- Justice Jugdish Singh Khehar is the present CJI.
- Advisory Jurisdiction refers to the process where the President seeks the court's advice on legal matters (Article 143).
- The Supreme Court is a court of record (Article 129).
- Under Article 139 (A) (inserted by the 44th Amendment), the Supreme Court may transfer to it self, cases from one or more High Court if these questions involve a significant question of law.

Comptroller and Auditor General (CAG Afticle 148-151)

- The Comptroller and Auditor General is appointed by the President under Article 148 of the Constitution.
- The CAG audits all receipts and expenditures of the Union and State Governments.
- The CAG also acts as the external auditor for the government-owned companies.
- The CAG submits its reports tot eh President (in case of accounts relating to the Union Government) or to the concerned State Governors (for State Government Accounts).
- The CAG is also the head of the Indian Audits and Accounts Service (IA & AS). The office of the CAG was established in 1860.
- The first CAG of India was V Narahari Rao (1948-1954).
- The CAG can only be removed from office in manner similar to a Judge of the Supreme Court.
- The salary and benefits of the CAG cannot be changed to his disadvantage

during his tenure.

- The CAG is not eligible for further office under the Union or State Governments. The expenses of the office of the CAG is charged to the Consolidated Fund of India.
- Attorney General of India
- The Attorney General is the highest law officer in the country appointed by the President under Article 79 of the Constitution.
- The Attorney General can participate in proceedings of the Parliament without the Right to Vote (Article 88)
- The First Attorney General, a candidate must be qualified to be appointed as a Judge of the Supreme Court..

Part VI

The States (Article 152-237)

The Governor

- The Governor is the Constitutional Head of the State and the same Governor can act as Governor of more than one State (Article 153).

Qualifications

- Must be a citizen of India.
- Completed 35 years of age.
- Shouldn't be member of either House of Parliament or State Legislature.
- Must not hold any office of profit.

- The Governor is appointed by the President (Article 155) and Article 156 states that the Governor holds office during the pleasure of the President.
- Article 161 gives the Governor the power to grant pardons, reprieves, remission of the punishment to persons convicted under the state law.
- Article 163 talks of discretionary powers of the Governor, which is not even provided to the President, Moreover, the courts cannot question his discretion.
- Article 171 states that the States where Legislative Councils exists, the Governor can nominate some members from amongst those distinguished in literature, science, art, cooperative movement and social service.
- Article 213 empowers the Governor to issue the ordinances during the recess of the State Legislature.

States Legislature

- Article 163 Council of Ministers to aid and advise the Governor.
- Article 165 An Advocate General for each of the State.
- Article 169 Abolition or creation of Legislative Councils in States.
- Most of the states have unicameral system, only 7 states have legisaltive council. These states are Andhra Pradesh, Bihar, Jammu & Kashmir, Karnataka, Maharashtra, Uttar Pradesh and Telangana.
- Legislative Assembly Legislative Assembly consists of Representative directly elected by the people. The strength of assembly varier from 60 to 500 members. However assembly of Sikkem, Goa, Mizoram, Arunacha Pradesh, Nagaland and Puducherry have less than 60 members.
- Composition of Legislative Council Unlike the members of the Legislative Assembly, the members of Legislative Council are indirectly elected. The maximum strength of the Council is fixed at one-third of the Total strength of assembly and the minimum strength is fixed at 40.

High Courts (Article 214-232)

There are 24 High Courts in India. The Calcutta High Court, established in 1862, is the oldest High Court in India. The Bombay and Madras High Courts were also established in the same year. The newest High Courts are the Tripura, Meghalaya and Manipur High Courts, all were established in the year 2013.

The Panchayats

(Article 243-243 O)

Introduced by the 73rd Amendment Act, 1992 which envisaged a three tier system of local government.

There

1. Gram panchayat at the village level
2. Panchayat Samiti at the block level
3. Zila Parishad at the district level

- The Panchayat system exists in all states

except Nagaland, Meghalaya and Mizoram. It also exists in all Union Territories except Delhi.

- Panchyat system is provided for all states having a population more than 2 million. Every Panchayat can continue for 5 years from the date of its first meeting.

The Municipalities (Article 243 P-243 G)

- Introduced by the 74th Amendment Act, 1992 which envisages three types of urban local bodies, namely, Nagar Panchayat, Municipal Council and Municipal Corporation.

Jurisdiction and Seats of High Courts

Court Name	Estd. in the year	Territorial Jurisdiction	Seat
Mumbai	1862	Maharashtra, Dadra and Nagar Haveli, Goa, Daman and Diu	Mumbai *(Bench at Nagpur, Panaji, and Aurangabad)*
Kolkata	1862	West Bengal, Andaman and Nicobar Islands	Calcutta *(Circuit bench at Port Blair)*
Chennai	1862	Tamil Nadu and Puducherry	Chennai *(Bench at Madurai)*
Allahabad	1866	Uttar Pradeh	Allahabad *(Bench at Lucknow)*
Kanataka	1884	Karnataka	Bangalore *(Circuit Benches at Hubli Dharwad and Gulbarga)*
Patna	1916	Bihar	Patna
Madhya Pradesh	1956	Madhya Pradesh	Jabalpur *(Benches at Gwalior and Indore)*
Jammu & Kashmir	1928	Jammu and Kashmir	Srinagar and Jammu
Punjab and Haryana	1875	Punjab, Haryana and Chandigarh	Chandigarh
Orissa	1948	Odisha	Cuttack
Guwahati	1948	Assam, Nagaland, Mizoram and Arunachal Pradesh	Guwahati *(Bench at Kohima, Aizwal and Itanagar)*
Rajasthan	1949	Rajasthan	Jodhpur *(Bench at Jaipur)*
Andhra Pradesh	1954	Andhra Pradesh, Telangana	Hyderabad
Kerala	1958	Kerala and Lakshadweep	Ernakulam
Gujarat	1960	Gujarat	Ahmedabad
Delhi	1966	National Capital Territory of Delhi	New Delhi
Himachal Pradesh	1971	Himachal Pradesh	Shimla
Sikkim	1975	Sikkim	Gangtok
Chhattisgarh	2000	Chhattisgarh	Bilaspur
Uttarakhand	2000	Uttarakhand	Nainital
Jharkhand	2000	Jharkhand	Ranchi
Tripura	2013	Tripura	Agartala
Manipur	2013	Manipur	Imphal
Meghalaya	2013	Meghalaya	Shillong

Name	Est.	Seat
Balwantrai Mehta	1957	Establish local bodies, devolve power and authority, unit of decentralised government to be Block/Samiti. Conceptualised PRIs as 3-tier system.
K Santhanam	1963	Panchaytats to have powers to levy tax on land revenue etc, Panchyati Raj Finance Corporation to be set-up.
Ashok Mehta	1978	District to be a viable administrative unit for planning, PRIs as two-tier system with Mandal Panchayat and Zila Parishad.
GVK Rao	1985	PRIs to be activated and supported, Block Development Office (BDO) to be central to rural development.
LM Singhvi	1986	Local self-governments to be constitutionally recognised, non-involvement of political parties.

- The first Municipal Corporation in India was introduced in Madras in 1688. The Madras Municipal Corporation is the first municipal body in the whole commonwealth outside the UK. The Bombay and Calcutta Corporations were established in 1726.
- Municipal Corporations are established in cities with population greater than 1 million.
- Nagar Panchayat administers urban areas having population greater than 30000 and less than 100000.
- A Municipal Council administers an urban area of population 200000 or less.

Relations between the Union and the States (Article 245-263)

- Legislative Relations
- Administrative Relations
- Financial Relations
- Article 262 Adjudication of disputes relating to waters of inter-state rivers or river valleys.
- Article 263 Inter-state council.

Finance, Property, Contracts and Suits (Article 264-300 A)

- Article 266 Consolidated Fund of India.
- Article 267 Contingency Fund of India.

Part IV

Services Under the Union and the States (Article 308-232)

- Article 312 All India Services.
- Article 315 Public Service Commissions for the Union and for the States.
- The first Public Service Commission was set-up in 1926, on the recommendations of the Lee Commission.
- The Government of India Act, 1935 provided for the establishment of the Federal Public Service Commission and Provincial Public Service Commissions.
- At least half of the members are civil servants with at least 10 years experience in central or state services.
- The tenure of each member is six years or upto the age of 65, whichever is earlier.

Unions Public Service Commission (UPSC)

- Constitution provides a Public Service Commission for the Union, a Public Service Commission for each state or a Joint Public Service Commission for a group of states.
- The appointment is done by the President in case of the Union or Joint Commission and by the Governor of the State in the case of a State Commission.
- Age of retirement for a member of UPSC in 65 years and for a member of PSC of a State or a Joint Commission is 62 years.
- Present Chairperson of UPSC is Alka Sirohi.

Funcions

- To conducts exams for appointment to service under the Union.
- Maintains continuity in administration.
- Members of UPSC can be removed by the President on the charges of misbehavior, it these charges arc upheld by the Supreme Court.

Elections (Article 324-329)

- Article 324 stipulates that the superintendence, direction and control of elections shall be vested in the Election Commission.
- Article 325 provides for a single electoral roll for every constituency. Also stipulates that no person shall be eligible or ineligible for inclusion in electoral rolls on the basis of race, religion, caste or sex.
- Article 326 stipulates that elections shall be held on the basis of adult suffrage. Every person, who is a citizen of India and is not less than 18 years of age shall be eligible for inclusion.

Political Parties

- There is no any discussion about political parties constitution.
- Registration of the People Act, 1951 provides for registration of political parties with the election commission.
- A political party shall be eligible to be recognised as a National party if
  - (i) It secures at least 6% of the valid votes polled in any four or more states, at a general election to the Houses of the People or to the State Legislative Assembly; and
  - (ii) In addition, it wins at least four seats in the House of the People from any State or States.

or

(iii) It wins at least 2% seats in the House of the People (i.e., 11 seats in the existing House having 543 members) and these members are elected from at least three different States.

Likewise, a political party shall be entitled to be recognised as a State party, if

(i) It secures at least 6% of the valid votes polled in the State at a general election, either to the House of the People or to be Legislative Assembly of the State concerned; and

(ii) In addition, it wins at least two seats in the Legislative Assembly of the State concerned.

or

It wins at least 3% of the total number of seats in the Legislative Assembly of the State or at least three seats in the Assembly, whichever is more.

Elections Commission

- The Election Commission is an autonomous, quasi-judiciary constitutional body. Its function is to conduct free and fair elections in India.
- The Election Commission was established on January 25, 1950 under Article 324 of the Constitution.
- The first Chief Election Commissioner was Sukumar Sen and the persent Chief Election Commissioner is Dr. Nasim Zaidi.

Planning Commission

- The Planning Commission was established in March 1950 by an executive resolution of the Government of India (i.e., Union Cabinet) on the recommendation of the Advisory Planning Board constituted in 1946 under the Chairmanship of KC Neogi.
- Now, the Planning Commission has been replaced by NITI Aayog.

NITI Aayog

- NITI Aayog or National institution for transforming India Aayog is a policy think-tank of Union Government of India and aims to involve the states in economic policy-making in India. It will be providing strategic and technical advice to the central and the State Governments.
- Prime Minister of India heads the Aayog as its Chairperson.

Present Members

The various members of NITI Aayog are

- **Chairperson :** Prime Minister Narendra Modi.
- **Vice-Chairperson** : Bibek Debroy
- **CEO :** Amitab Kant
- **Ex-officio members :** Rajnath Singh, Arun Jaitley, Suresh Prabhu adn Radha Mohan Singh.
- **Special Invites :** Nitin Godkari, Smrite Zubin Irani and Thawar Chand Gehlot.
- **Full-time members :** Bibek Debray, VK Saraswat, Ramesh Chand.

Governing Council: All CMs and Lieutenant Governors of UTs.

National Development Council (NDC)

- Functions of the NDC was to review the working of national plan. The NDC was formed in 1952, to associate the states in the formulation of the plans.
- The PM is the ex-officio chairman of NDC.
- It is an extra-constitutional and extra legal body.

Finance Commission

- Article 280 of the Constitution of India provide for a Finance Commission as a quasi-judicial body. It is constituted by the President of India every fifth year.
- It consists of Chairman and 4 other members.

Functions: The Finance Commission is required to make recommendation to the President of India in the following matters, The distribution of the net proceeds of taxes to be shared between the centre and the states and the allocation between the state, the respective shares of such proceeds. The 14th Finance Commission was appointed on 2nd January, 2013 under the Chairmanship of YV Reddy.

Amendments of the Constitution (Article 368)

Three methods for amendment of different provisions of the Constitution are

1. Simple Majority in both the Houses of Parliament.
2. Article requiring ratification of the one-half member of the concerned Legislative Assembly and passed by the total membership of the each House of the Parliament and majority not less than 2/3 of the members present and voting in the House.
3. Provisions requiring passing by total membership of the each House of the Parliament and majority not less than two-third of the members present and voting in each House.

It has been held by the Supreme court in the Kashavananda Bharati Case (1973) that every provision of the Constitution is amendable under the meaning of Article 368 except the basic features of the Constitution.

e-Governance

The word electronic in the terms e-governance implies technology driven governance.

The perspective of the e-governance is "the use of the technology that both governing and have to be governed."

Generally five basic models are given in e-Governance

- G2C (Government to Citizens)
- G2B (Government to Business)
- G2E (Government to Employees)
- G2G (Government to Governments)
- C2G (Citizen to Governments)

The National e-Governance Place (NeGP) takes a holistic view of e-governance initiatives across the country, integrating them into a collective vision.

Impacts of e-Governance

e-Governance brings about two major impacts firstly, making the government office work smart. Secondly, e-governance makes services available to the citizen at his doorstep through the internet.

Some of the most successful citizen oriented e-governance projects are the Railways Reservation System, MCA 21 is the Ministry of Corporate Affairs and Bhoomi Project in Andhra Pradesh, etc.

E-districts

It is a mission mode under e-governance. Its objective under National E-Governance Policy is the computerisation of services. Under it, different programmes are conducted in following states

- Jandoot Project-Madhya Pradesh
- Compact 2020-Andhra Pradesh
- Land Programme-Karnataka
- Friends-Kerala
- Disha-Haryana

PARLIAMENTARY TERMS

- **Quorum** It is the minimum number of members required to transact the business of the House. Article 100 of the Constitution specific that the Quorum of the either House shall be 10% of the strength of the House.
- **Question** Hour The first hour of every sitting of Parliament of called the Question Hour. Questions usually need a 10 day notice before being answered by the concerned minister.
- **Starred Questions** To be answered orally on the floor of the House. Supplementary questions can be asked.
- **Unstarred Questions** To be answered in writing. No supplementary questions may be asked.
- Zero Hour Does not formally exist in the Parliamentary procedure. The hour after Question Hour is popularly known as Zero Hour. Members raise matters which type fell urgent.
- **Adjournment Motion** Motion to adjoum the proceedings to the House, so as to take up a matter of urgent public importance. It can be moved by any member. Required support form at least

50 members.

- **Calling Attention Motion** A no Confidence Motion the attention of a Minister to an urgent matter and the Minister may make a statement regarding it.
- **No Confidence Motion** A No Confidence Motion indicates lack of confidence of the Lok Sabha in the Council of Ministers. It can be introduced int the Lok Sabha only. If the Motion is passed, the government must resign.

CONSTITUTIONAL AMENDMENTS

- First Amendment Act, 1951 Added Ninth Schedule.
- Seventh Amendment Act, 1956
- Necessitated on account of reorganisation of States on a linguistic basis.
- Fifteenth Amendment Act, 1963 Age of retirement of the Judges of High Court has been extended from 60 to 65 years.
- Twenty Sixth Amendment Act, 1971 Abolished the titles and special privileges of former rulers of princely states.
- Thirty Sixth Amendment Act, 1975 Made Sikkem a State.
- Forty Fourth Amendment Act, 1978 The Right to Property was deleted from Part III. Article 352 was amended to provide 'Armed Rebellion' as one of the circumstances for declaration of emergency.
- Seventy Third Amendment Act, 1992 The institution of Panchayati Raj receive constitutional guarantee, status and legitimacy, XIth Schedule was added to deal with it. It also inserted Part IX, containing Article, 243, 243 A to 243 O.
- Eighty Ninth Amendment Act, 2003 the Act adds Article 338 A and provides for creation of National Commission for Scheduled Tribes.
- Ninety Third Amendment Act, 2005 To reserve seats for socially and educationally backward classes, besides the Scheduled Caste and the Scheduled Tribes, in private unaided institutions other than those run by minorities.
- Ninety Fifth Amendment Act, 2009 Extends the reservation of seats for SC/ST in the Lok Sabha for another 10 years. In Article 334 of the Constitution, for the words 'sixty years', the words 'seventy years' was substituted.
- Ninety Seventh Amendment Act, 2011 Amendment of Article 19(1)(i), Insertion of Article 43B, Insertion of Part IXB. This amendment gives constitutional status to cooperatives.
- Ninety Eighth Amendment Act, 2012 (Insert Article 371 J) To empower the Governor of Karnataka to take steps to develop Hyderabad-Karnataka Region.
- Ninety-Ninth Amendment Act, 2014 deals with replacing the collegium system for the appointments of the Judges of the Supreme Court and the 24 High Courts. But Supreme Court of India has declared this unconstitutional and void.
- One Hundred Amendment Act, 2015 to give effect to the acquiring of territories by India and transfer of certain territories to Bangladesh in pursuance of the agreements and its protocol.
- One Hundred One Amendment Act, 2016 Goods and Services Tax Bill.
- One Hundred Two Amendment Act, Constitutional status to National Commission for Backward Classes.
- One Hundred Third Amendment Act, 10% reservation to the poor among general category

INDIAN HISTORY

ANCIENT INDIA

PRE-HISTORY PERIOD

Paleolithic Period

- Pre-History, means literally 'before history', it beings with the appearance of human being.
- Homo sapiens first appeared towards the end of this phase.
- In this period, man barely managed to gather his good and subsisted on hunting.
- Distinguished by the development of the first stone tools made up of Quartzite.
- The archaeological stone of Bore (Maharashtra) is oldest site found with stone age evidences.
- Paleolithic period is divided into three phase. They are
  1. Lower Palaeolithic
  2. Middle Palaeolithic
  3. Upper Palaeolithic

Mesolithic Period

- Domestication of animals (particularly, dogs) began and characteristic tools were used, called as microliths.
- Bhimbetka in Madhya Pradesh, is known for ancient caves depicting pictures of birds, animals and humans.

Neolithic Period

- Neolithic period knew about fire and wheel.
- An important site o this age and Burzahom, which mea s 'the place of birch.'

Chalcolithic Period

- Use fo Copper and Stone made tools.
- They practiced agriculture, venerated Mother Goddess and worshipped the bull.
- Excavation at Koldihwa has revealed evidence of those three periods of pre-history in India.

Indus Valley Civilisation

- Indus Valley Civilisastion or is one of the four earliest civilisations of the world.
- According to radiocarbon dating, initiation of Indus Valley Civilisation can be dated around 2500-1750 BC.
- Systematic town planning was based on grid system; burnt bricks were used to construct houses; well-managed drainage system; Fortified citadel, highly urbanised; absence of iron implements.
- The towns were divided into 2 parts; the Upper Part or Citadel and the Lower Part. Harappans were ruled by a class of merchants, as no evidence of weapons are found there.
- The Great Bath (Mohenjodaro) was used for religious bathing. There were changing rooms alongside.
- Six granaries in a row were found in the Citadel at Harappa.
- Indus people sowed seeds in November and reaped their harvest in April, because of the danger of flood.
- Produced Cotton, Gram, Wheat, Barley, Rai, Peas, Seasum, Rice and Mustard.
- Indus people first produced cotton, which the Greeks termed as Sindon (derived form Sindh)
- Animals known were oxen, sheep, buffaloes, goats, pigs, elephants, dogs, cats, asses and camels. Horse and Cow was not known to Harappans.
- Weli-knit external and internal trade. Barter system was prevalent.
- A very interesting feature of this civilisation was that iron was not known to the people.
- The Indus people used weights and measures in the multiples of 16.
- Harappans looked on Earth as fertility Goddess and phallic (lingam) and yoni worship was prevalent.
- Unicorn was the most worshipped

animals. Many trees (pipal), animals (bull), birds (dove, pigeon) and stones too were worshipped though no evidence of temple has been found.

- The Seal of Pashupati depicts elephant, tiger, rhinoceros and buffalo. Two deers appear at the feet of Pashupati.
- The Indus people believed in ghosts and evil forces evident by their use of amulets for protection against them. Fire altars are found at Lothal and Kalibangan.
- Dead bodies were placed in North-South orientation.
- The greatest artistic creation of the Harappan culture were the seals, made of steatite. Harappan script is pictographic, but hasn't been deciphered yet.
- The script was written from right to left line and left to right in the second line. this style is called Boustrophedon.
- Occupations practiced were spinning, weaving, boat-making, goldsmith, making pottery and seal-making.
- The possible causes of the decline of the civilisation may be invasion of the Aryans, recurrent floods, social break-up of Harappans and earthquakes etc.
- Dholavira is the largest Harappan site in India. It situated in Gujarat.
- Boundaries North-Mandu (J&K); South-Daimabad (Maharashtra); East-Alamgripur; West-Sutkagendor.

Indus Valley Sites

Site	Discovery/Finding(s)
Harappa	Situated on river Ravi in Montgomery district of Punjab (Pakistan). It was excavated by Daya Ram Sahni in 1921-23. The Indus Civilisation is named after it as the Harappan Civillisation Stone dancing Natraja and Cemetry-37 have been found here.
Chanhudaro (Sindh, Pakistan)	On river Indus, discovered by NG Majumdar (1931), only Indus site without citadel; bronze figurines of bullock cart and ekkas; a small pot suggesting a kink well.
Mohenjodaro (Mound of Dead)	Situated on river Indus in Larkana distr ct of Sind (pak). It was excavated by RD Bannerji in 1922. The main building includes the Great Bath the Great Granary, the Collegiate Building and the Assembly Hall. The dancing girl made of bronze has been found here Pashupati Mahadeva/proto Shiva seal; fragment of woven cotton, etc are other findingss
Lothal (Gujarat)	Discovered by SR Rao (1951) situated on river Bhogava. A part or the town was divided into citadel and the over town and the lower town and dockyard Evidence of type has been found here.
Kalibangan (Meaning, Black Bangles) (Rajasthan)	Discovered by BB Lal (1961); situated on Ghaggar river a ploughed field, a wooden furrow; seven fire-altars bones of camel; anc evidence of two types of burials namely—circular grave and rectangular grave.
Dholavira	It was found on river Luni of Kachchh district in Gujarat. Largest and latest site discovered by JP Joshi (1967-68). It has a unique water management system only site to be divided into 3 parts largest Harappan inscription and a stadium.
Surkotada (Gujarat)	Discovered by JP Joshi on 1972; evidence of horse found; oval grave; pit burials and seemingly a port city.

Banawali (Haryana)	On river Sarasrweati; discovered by RS Bisht (1931), evidence of both pre-Harappan and Hrarappan culture, lacked systematic drainage system evidence of good quality barley

VEDIC PERIOD

Rig Vedic Period (1500-1000 BC)

- Aryans were the said to be propounders of vedic civilisation. They spoke a language called arya.
- The Aryans were semi-nomadic pastoral people and originally believed to have lived somewhere in the Steppers, stretching form Southern Russia to Central Asia.
- The whole region in which the Aryans were first Settled in India was called the Land of 7 Rivers or Sapta Sindhawa.

Political Organisation

- The Dasrajan War Battle of 10 kings against Sudas (Bharata king of Tritsus) on the bank of river Parushni.
- Sudas emerged victorious. It was mainly a tribal system of government in which the military element was strong.
- Traces of election of the King by the assembly, called Samiti.
- Villages were headed by Gramini.
- In day-to-day administration, the King was assisted by the Purohita (most important), a Senani and Vrata, Gana, Grama and Sardha (tribal groups performing various military functions.)
- Tribe was know as Jana and its king as Rajan.

Society

- People were loyal to the tribe, called Jana (mentioned 275 times in the Rigveda) as kingdom/territory was not yet established. Women enjoyed freedom and respect.

Economy

- No regular revenue system, kingdom maintained by voluntary tribute called bali and booty won in battles.
- Aryan's main occupation was mainly pastoral. Agriculture was a secondary occupation.
- Cow was a standard unit of exchange. Gold coins-Nishka, Krishnal and Satmana.
- The staple crop was Yava (barely).

Religion

- Worshipped Nature, Indra (also called Purandara-breaker of forts) was the most important divinity.
- Soma was considered to be the Good of plants.
- People worshped the divinities mainly for Praja (children), Pashu (cattle), food, health and wealth. No temple or idol worship was noted.

Rigvedic Terms

Term	Meaning
Dasyus	Original inhabitant of India
Ayas	Copper/bronze
Vajrapati/ Kalapas	Officer enjoying authority over large tract of land.
Gramini	Head of the village
Gavisthi	Fighting hordes, Search for cows/war for cows

Rigvedic Rivers

River	Name in Rigveda
Indus	Sindhu
Kurrma	Krumu
Jhelum	Vitasta
Chenab	Asikni
Ravi	Parushini
Beas	Vipasa
Sutlej	Sutudri
Gomati	Gomal
Saraswati	Sarasvati
Ghaggar	Drishadavati

Later Vedic Period (1000-500 BC)

- In this period, Aryans expanded form Punjab over the whole of Western Uttar Pradesh covered by the Ganga-Yamuna Doab.

Political Organisation

- King (Samrat) became more powerful and tribal authority tended to become territorial.
- King's position strengthened by rituals like Ashwamedha and Vajapeya Yajnas.

Society

- Society was clearly divided into four varnas—Brahmana, Kshatriya, Vaishya and Shudra. Position of women deteriorated. The institution of Gotra (descent from common ancestors) appeared for the first time.

Religion

- Prajapati became the superme God, followed by Rudra (animal God) and Lord Vishnu (preserver and protector or people).
- Idolatry began in this period.
- Pushana, who looked after the cattles was 'God of Shudras'.
- Sacrifices, rather than prayers, became more important.

Economy

- Beginning of town and settled life.
- Agriculture was the main livelihood.
- Wheat and rice (called vrihi in later Vedic texts) became the staple crop.
- Occupations like those of ironsmith, coppersmith, jewel workers and weaving, were reserved for women.

Vedic Literature

The Vedas

- Rigveda the oldest Indo-European language text is a collection of hymns. Contains 1028 hymns and 10 mandalas. The 10th Mandala contains four varnas or the Purushasukta hymn, whereas 3rd Mandala contains Gayatri mantra, which was compiled in the praise of Sun God.
- Samaveda Collection of melodies, contains Dhrupad raga. It is a book of chants.
- Yajurveda Contains hymns and rituals/ sacrifices.
- Atharvaveda Charms and spells to ward-off evils and diseases.

The Brahmanas

- Contains ritualistic formulae and explains the social and religious meaning of rituals. Each veda has several Brahmanas attached to it.
  - Rigveda :Kaushitaki and Aitareya
  - Yajurveda :Taittiriya and Satapatha
  - Samaveda :Panchvish and Jemineya
  - Atharvaveda :Gopatha

The Arnyakas

- The word Aranya means the forest. These texts were called Aranyakas, because they were written mainly by the hermits and students living in the jungle.

The Upanishadas

- Philosophical texts emphasising value of right belief and knowledge; criticising rituals/sacrifices; There are 108 upanishadas. Brihadaranyaka is the oldest upanishada.

Smritis

- Explains rules and regulations in Vedic life. These are Manusmriti (the first law book); naradasmriti, Yajnavalkyasmriti and Parasharasmriti.

Vedangas

- These are Limbs of Vedas and are six in number
- Shiksha (Pronunciation)
- Kalpa (Rituals)
- Vyakaran (Grammar)
- Nikrukta (Explanation)
- Chhanda (Metrics)
- Jyotish (Astrology)

Upavedas

There are four Upavedas

Upaveda	Deals with	Upaveda of
Dhanurveda	Art of warfare	Yajurveda
Gandharva-veda	Art and music	Samaveda
Shilpaveda	Architecture	Atharvaveda

Darshana

There are six schools of Indian philosophy, called Shada-darshana.

These are

Nyaya Darshana	Gautam
Vaishesika Darshana	Kanada
Sankhya Darshana	Kapila
Yoga Darshana	Patanjali
Purva Mimansa	Jamini
Uttara Mimansa	Badrayna or (Vyasa)

Epics

- Mahabharata by Ved Vyasa, also called Jaya Samhita and Satasahasri Samhita has 100000 verses and are older than Ramayana, written by Valmiki, and has 29000 verses.

Mahajanapadas

Mahajanapada	Capital
- Kashi	Varanasi
- Anga	Champanagri
- Vajji	Vaishali
- Chedi	Suktimati
- Kuru	Hastinapur
- Matsya	Viratnagar
- Assaka	Budanya
- Gandhara	Taxila
- Kosala	Sharavasti
- Magadh	Rajagriha
- Malla	Kushinagar
- Vatsa	Kaushambi
- Panchala	Ahichhatra
- Surasena	Mathura
- Avanti	Ujjain
- Kamboja	Rajpur

JAINISM AND BUDDHISM

- The main causes being the reaction against domination of Brahamans and spread fo agricultural economy in the North-East.
- Came into existence around 600 BC.

Jainism

- Founded by Rishabhadeva (Emblem : Bull) born in Ayodhya.
- There were 24 tirthankaras (great teachers), the 23rd being Parshvanatha and the 24th being the Vardhamana Mahavira.
- Mahavira was born in 540 BC in Kundagram near Vaishali.
- Father Siddhartha of Jantrika Kshatriya Clan.
- Mother Trishala—sister of Lichchhavi Chief Chetaka, merried to Yoshada and had a daughter named Priyadarshini, whose husband Jamali became his first disciple.
- Mahavira became an ascetic at the age of 30, attained Kaivalya (Jina) outside the town of Jimbhikgrama at the age of 42 and and died at the age of 72 in 468 BC in Pavapuri near Nalanda (Bihar).
- Five Doctrines of Jainism
  1. Do not commit violence (Ahimsa)
  2. Do not steal (Asteya)
  3. Do not acquire property (Aparigraha)
  4. Do not speak lie (Satya)
  5. Observe continence (Brahmacharya)
- Triratans of Jainism are right knowledge, right faith and right conduct.
- Jainism says salvation is possible only by abandoining all possessions, along curse of fasting, self mortification, study and meditation.
- Jainism recongnised existence of God, but lower than Jina. It didn't condemn verna system unlike Buddhism.
- Jainism was divided into two sects after Vallabhi Council, Svetambaras (wearing white dresses) under Sthulbhadra and Digambaras (naked) under Bhadrabahu.
- Jaina texts were written in Prakrit language.
- Jainsm could not delink clearly from brahmanical religion, hence field to attract masses; admitted both men and women. Jain monastic establishments were called basadis.
- Jainism was patronised by Kharavela–the king of Kalinga; Chandraputa Mourya become the disciple of Bhadrabhau and spread Jainism in the South.

Councils

- First Council (300 BC), At Pataliputra Under Sthulbhadra (Pataliputra) Jaina Canons compiled.
- Second Council (AD 5th Century), Under Kshamasramana (Vallabhi) 12 Angas and 12 Upangas were compiled in Prakrit (Ardh Magadhi) language.

Buddhism

- Founded by Gautama Buddha, also known as Siddhartha or Sakyamuni or Tatagata.
- Born in 563 BC in Lumbini (Nepal) in Shakya Kshatriya Clan.
- His father Suddhodana was a Saka ruler and his mother Mahamaya of Kosalan dynasty died early. Brought up by step mother Gautami.
- Married with Yashodhara and had a son Rahul.
- Triratnas in Buddhism stand for 3 pillars
  - — Buddha Its founder
  - — Dhamma His teachings
  - — Sangha Order of Buddhist monks and nuns

The Dhamma

The Four Great Truths

- The world is full is sorrow and misery.
- The cause of all pain the misery is desire.
- Pain and misery can be ended by killing or controlling desire.
- Desire can be controlled by following the Eight-Fold Path.

The Eight-Fold Path

1. Right Understating	1. Right Efforts
2. Right Thought	2. Right Speech
3. Right Action	3. Right mindfulness
4. Right Livelihood	4. Right concentration

Belief in Nirvana

- When desire ceases, rebirth ceases and nirvana is attained i.e., freedom from the cycle of birth, death and rebirth is gained by following Eight-fold path.

Belief in Ahimsa

- On should not cause injury to any living being or animal.

Law of Karma

- Man reaps the fruits of his past deeds.

Buddhist Literature

- In Pali langauage commonly referred to as Tripitakas, i.e., 'three fold basket'.
- Vinaya Pitaka Rules of discipline in Buddhist monasteries.
- Sutta Pitaka It contains collection of Buddha's sermons and teachings. It is largest among all three pitakas.
- Abhidhamma Pitaka Explanation of the philosophical principles of the Buddhist religion. Mahavamsha and Dipavamsa are the other Buddhist texts or Sri Lanka.
- Causes of Decline of Buddhism
- Use of Sanskrit, the langauge of intellectuals, in place of Pali, the language of the common people. Revival of Hinduism.

Buddhist Councils

Buddhist Counicls	Period	Place	Chairman	Patron
First	483 BC	Rajagriha	Mahankashyapa	Ajatashutru
Second	383 BC	Vaishali	Subakami	Kalashoka
Third	250 BC	Patliputra	Mogaliputta Tiss	Ashoka
Fourth	AD 72	Kundalvana	Vasumitra, Ashwaghosa	Kanishka

DYNASTIES OF ANCIENT INDIA

Haryanka Dynasty

- Bimbisara was the founder, who expanded to Magadha kindom by annexing Anga, and entering into matrimonial alliances with Kosala and Vaishali. He was contemporary of Buddha. Capital-Rajgir (Girivraja).

- He was the first King, whom Mahantma Buddha gave sermon and Converted into Buddhism.
- Ajastashatru came to power by killing his father. Annexed Vaishali, Kosala and Lichhavi kingdom.
- Udayin founded the new capital, Pataliputra.

Shinsunaga Dynasty

- Founded by Shishunaga; Kalashoka or Kakavarin convened the Second Buddhist Council. Their greatest achievement was the destruction of Avanti.

Nanda Dynasty

- Considered as non-Kshatriyan dynasty, founded by Mahapadma Nanda. Alexander atacked during Dhana Nanda's reign. Cyrus was the first foreign invader of India.
- Alexander, the king of Macedonia, invaded India in 326 BC and fought the Battle of Hydapses (Jhelum) with Porus (Purushottam) of Paurava dynasty.

Mauryan Dynasty

- Important rulers of Mauryan Dynasty are

Chadragupta Maurya

(321-298 BC)

- The first ruler who overthrew the Nanda dynasty with the help of Chanakya.
- He has been called Sandrocottus and Androcottus by Greek scholars.
- Chadragupta Maurya defeated Seleucus Nikator the general of Alexander (304 BC), who later sent Megasthenese the author of Indica to Chadragupta's court.
- His mother was Mura—a Shudra woman in Nanda's court.
- He adopted Jainism and went to Sravanabelgola with Bhadrabahu.

Bindudara (298-273 BC)

- He was called Amitraghat (i.e., slayer of foes) by Greek writers; Greek ambassador, Deimachos visited his court; said to conquer the land between the two seas—The Arabian Sea and Bay of Bengal.
- Bindusara appointed his eldest son Sushom as his viceroy at Taxila and Ashoka at Ujjain.

Ashoka (293-273 BC)

- For the first eight years Ashoka ruled like a cruel king and maintained discipline.
- He was called Devanamapriya, Dear to Gods.
- The name of Ashoka occurs only in copies of Minor Rock Edict I.
- Languages (scripts) used on inscription—Brahmi and Karoshthi (North-Western India) and Greek (Afghanistan) script deciphered by James Princep (in AD 1837).
- Ashoka was the first king to maintain direct contact with people through inscriptions.
- Kalinga War (261 BC) mentioned in 13th Major Rock Edict converted Ashoka to Buddhism under Upaguta.
- Sanchi Stupa was built by Ashoka.
- The last Mauryan king Brihadratha, was killed by Pushymitra Sung in 185 BC, who established the Sunga dynasty.
- The Punch-marked coins carring the symbol of the peacock and the hill and crescent, famed the imperial currency of Mauryas.
- Ringwells for domestic use fo water appeared first under the Mauryas.
- Sri Lanka is called Tamraparni in the Ashokan inscription.

The Indo-Greeks

- The most famous king among the Indo-Greeks was Menander (165-145 BC) also called Milinda, his capital was Sakala (modern Sialkot) in Punjab.
- Converted to Buddhism by Nagasena as per the Milidapanho—a Pali text.
- The Greeks were the first to issue coins attributable to the king and also the first to issue gold coins in India; introduced Hellenistic art.

The Shakas

- The most famous ruler was Rudradaman I (AD 130-150), who repaired Sudarshana lake in Kathiawar region, issued first ever inscription in Sanskrit (Junagarh inscription). He defeated the Satavahanas twice.
- Vikramaditya, the king of Ujjain, was the only one who defeated the Shakas. To commemorate the victory, he started the Vikarm Samvat in 57 BC.

- The Parthians The most famous king was Gondophernes (AD 19-45), in whose reign St. Thomas visited India to propagate Christianity.

The Kushanas

- Also Called Yechi or Tocharians, were nomadic people from the Steppes.
- Kanishka was to greatest of the Kushanas, who started the Saka Era in AD 78.
- Kushanas were the first rulers to issue gold coins on a wide scale known for metallic purity.
- In the royal court of Kanishka, a host of scholars found patronage, like Parsave, Vasumitra, Asvaghosha, Nagarjuna, Charak (Physician) and Mathara.

The Sunga Dynasty (185-73 BC)

- The Sung Dynasty was established by Pushyamitra Sunga.
- They were basically Brahmins. This period saw the revival of Bhagvatism.
- Patanjali worte 'Mahabhasys' at this time.
- It arts, the Bharhut stupa is the most famous monument of the Sunga period.

The Kanva Dynasty (73-28 BC)

- In 73 BC, Devabhuti, the last ruler of the Sunga dynasty, was murdered by this minister Vasudeva, who usurped the throne and founded the Kanva dynasty replaced by the Satavahanas.

The Satavahanas (or Andhras)

- Simuka (60-73 BC) was the founder of the Satavahana dynasty.
- Satavahanas were finally succeeded by the Ikshvakus in AD 3rd century.
- Under the Satavahanas, many chaityas (worship halls) and viharas (monastries) were cut out from rocks mainly in North-West Deccan or Maharashtra the famous examples were Nasik, Kanaheri and Karle.
- The official language of the Satavahanas was Prakrit.
- The Satavahanas issued coins of lead (mainly), copper, bronze and potin.
- Gautamiputra Satakarni was a famous king.

The Pandyas

- Their capital was Madurai famous for pearls. The Pandyas were first mentioned by Megasthenese.
- Traded with Roman empire, sent embassies to emperor Augustus.

The Cholas

- The Chola kingdom, also called as Cholamandalam was situated to the North-East of Pandya Kingdom between Pennar and Vellar rivers.
- Their Capital was Kaveripattanam/Puhar.

The Cheras

- Their capital was Vanji (also called Kerala country). It has important trade relations with the Romans.

Sangam Age

- Sangam Age correspondsj to the post-Mauryan and Gupta periods.
- Sangam was a college or an assembly or Tamil poets, held under Royal Patronage.
- There Sangamas were held
  (i) at Maduari chaired by Agastya.
  (ii) at Kapatpuram, chaired by Tolkappiyar.
  (iii) at Maduri, chaired by Nakkirar.
- Kural by Tiruvalluvar is called the 'Fifth Vada' or 'the Bible of Tamil Land.'

Gupta Period

- The important rulers of Gupta period are

Chandragupta I (AD 319-334)

- Married a Lichchhavi princess, who strengthened his position and enhanced the prestige of the Guptas.
- He was the first Gupta ruler to acquire the title of Maharajadhiraja.
- Chadragupta IO was able the establish his authority over Magadha, Prayaga and Saketa.

Sumudragupta (AD 335-380)

- he is called the Napoleon of India (By VA Smith) on account of his conquests.
- Meghavarman the ruler of Sri Lank, sent a missionary to his court for permission to built a Buddhist temple at Gaya.
- The Allabhad pillar inscription gives detailed information about Samudragupta, it was composed by his court poet Harisena.
- His assumed the titles of Kaviraj and Vikrama.

- Chadragupta II (AD 380-414)
- Mehrauli inscription on Iron Pillar near Qutub Minar is related to him.
- His court was adorned by Navratnas, the chief being Kalidasa and Amarshimha.
- Fe-hien, Chines Pilgrim (AD 399-144) visited during his reign.
- Defeated Sakka Kshatrapa Rudrasimha III
- Chandragupta II also succeeded in Killing Rangupta, and not only seized his kingdom, but also married his widow Dhruvadevi.
- The Gupta age is called golden age of Indian history and saw the issuance of the largest number of gold coins.

Kamaragupta I (AD 415-455)

- Chadragupta II was succeeded by his son Kumargupta I.
- Kumargupta was the worshipper of God Kartikeya.
- He founded the 'Nalanda Mahavihara' which developed into a great centre of learning.

Skandagupta (AD 455-467)

- Skanndagupta was the last great ruler of the Gupta dynasty.
- During his reign the Gupta empire was invaded by the Hunas.

Pushyabhuti Dynasty

(AD 606-647)

- The greatest king was Harshavardhana, son of Prabhakar Vardhana of Thaneshwer. He shifted the capital to Kannauj.
- Hieun Tsang visited during his reign.
- He established a large monastery at Nalanda. Banabhata adorned his 4court, wrote Harshacharita and Kadambri harsha himself wrote three plays—Priyadarshika, Ratnawali and Nagananda.

Rashtrakutas

- Founded by Dantidurg; Krshna I buili the Kailasha temple at Ellora. Amoghavarsha, who is compared to Vikramaditya, wrote the first Kannada poetry Kaviraj Marg. Rashtrakutas are credited for building cave shrine Elephanta, dedicated to Shiva.

Gangas

- Rules Orissa; Narsimhadeva constructed the Sun Temple at Konark; Anantvarman built the Jagannath Temple at Puri; and Kesaris, who used to rule before Gangas build the Lingaraja Temple at Bhubaneshwar.

Pallavas

- Founder–Simhavishnu; Capital–Kanchi; greatest king Narsimhavarman, who founded the town of Mamallapuram (Mahabalipuram) and built rock-cut rathas and even pagodas.
- Palas, with their capital at Monghyr is kown for Dharmapla, their second king, who founded the Vikramashila University and revived the Nalanda University.
- The greatest ruler of Pratihars was Bhoja (also known as Mihir, Adivraha.)
- Khajuraho temples were built during the reign of Chandellas of Bundelkhand.
- Chalukyas of Vatapi-founded by Jayasimha were contemporary to Harshavardhan.
- Rajputs divided into four clans : Pratihars (S Rajasthan), Chauhans (E Rajasthan), Chalukyas/Solankis (Kathiawar), Parmars (Malwa).

The Cholas

- Founder Vijayalaya, Capital Tanjore.
- Aditya I wiped out the Pallavas and weakened the Pandyas.
- Purantaka I captured Madurai, but was defeated by the Rashtrakuta ruler Krishna III at the Battle of Takkolam.
- Rajaraja I (AD 985-1014) led a naval expedition against Shilendra empire (Malays Peninsula) and conquered Northern Sri Lanka; constructed Rajarajeshwari (or Brihadeshvara) Shiva temple at Tanjore.
- Rajendra I (AD 1014-1044) annexed the whole of Sri Lanka; took the title of Gangaikonda and founded Gangaikonda Cholapuram.
- Dancing Figure or Shiva (Nataraja) belongs to the Chola period. Local self government existed.

MEDIEVAL INDIA

- Mahammad bin Qasim invaded India in AD 712 and conquered Sindh.
- Sultan Mahmud of Ghazni led about 17 expeditions of India.
- In 1025, he attacked and raided the most celebrated Hindu temple of Somnath, situated on the sea coast of Kathiawar.

Foundation of the Delhi Sultanate

- Mohammad Ghori invaded India and was defeated by Prithviraj Chauhan in First Battle of Tarain (1191).
- Ghori defeated the Rajput king in Second Battle of Tarain (1192) and laid the foundation the Muslim dominion the India. He may be considered the 'founder of Muslim rule' in India.

Illbari Dynasty (AD 1206-1290)

Qutab-ud-in-Aibak

- Capital Lahore (initial); Delhi (later)
- The founder of the Slave dynasty. Also called Lakh Baksh because of his generosity.
- Gutub-ud-din-Aibak laid the foundation of Qutub Minar, after the name of the famous Sufi saint Khwaja Qutubuddin Bakhtiyar Kaki; built Quwwat-ul-Islam (first mosque in India) and Adhai Din ka Jhopra (Ajmer).
- Died while playing Chaugan (polo).

Iltutmish (AD 1210-1236)

- Attack of Mongols; formed Turkan-e-Chanalgani or Chalisa (a group of 40 powerful Turkish nobles).
- Divided his empire into Iqtas (assignment of land in lieu of salary).
- Introduced 2 types of coins-silver tanks and copper jital.

Razia Sultan (AD 1236-1240)

- First and last Muslim woman ruler of Medieval India.
- She disregarded Purdah, married Altunia, the Governor of Bhatinda.
- Bahram Shah, son of Iltutmish, killed her.

Balban (AD 1266-1286)

- Separated Military Department (Diwan-e-Ariz) and Finance Department (Diwan-e-Wazarat).
- he declared that king was the deputy of God (Niyabat-e-Khudai) and shadow of God (Zjl-e-Illahi) and introduced the practices of Sijdah or Paibos.

Khalji Dynasty (AD 1290-1320)

- Jalaluddin Firuz Khalji was the first ruler, who reviewed that India cannot be a totally Islamic state.
- Alauddin Khalji His conquests were that of Gujarat ruled by Vaghela king; Ranthambhor, Chittor and Malwa and later to the South (mainly by Malik Kafur).
- He abolished Zamindari in Khalisa land. No iqta was allotted in Doab area.
- Alauddin adopted the policy of Blood and Iron tin tackling the Mangols.
- He built Khizrabad, Alai Darwaja and his capital city Siri.
- Also built Hauz Khas in Delhi and added entrance door to Qutub Minar, introduced market reforms.
- Built a permanent army introduced Chehra and Dagh System.
- First Turkish Sultan who separated religion form politics.
- His court poets were Amir Khusrau and Mir Hassan Dehivi.

Tuglaq Dynasty (AD 1320-1413)

- Founded by Ghiyasuddin Tughlaq, who built the fortified city of Tughlaqabad and made it his capital.
- He was the first sultan to start irrigation works.
- Muhammad-bin-Tughlaq also called the wise fool king on account of five experiments, namely (a) Transfer of capital ot Daulatabad (b) Taxation in Doab (c) Qarachil expedition (d) Khurasan expedition (e) Token currency.
- The Sultan set-up a separate department Diwan-i-kohi. He gave Sondhar loans to farmers.
- South Indian states of the Vijayanagara empire, the Bahmani kingdom and the Sultanate of Madura were founded.
- Firoz Shah Tuglaq built new towns of Hissar, Firozpur, Fatehabad, Jaunpur and Firozabad (his capital). During his reign

two Ashokan pillars, one from Topara in Ambala and the other from Meerut were brought. Built canals was found of slaves are wrote a book Fatuhat Firozshahi.

- He repaired Qutub Minar when it was struck by lightening.
- Firoz Shah Tughlaq also made Iqtadari system hereditary and imposed new taxes like Kharaj (land tax equal to one-tenth of the producer) and Zakat and Khams (one-tenth of the booty captured in war).
- He made Jizya a separate tax and he imposed this tax upon the Brahmans for the first time in the history of Sultanate.
- He introduced the following coins— Aadha, Bhikh, Shashgani and Histragani.
- Timur Mongol leader of Central Asia, ordered general massacre in Delhi (AD 1398) at the time of Nasiruddin Mahmud (later Tuglaq king).

Sayyids and Lodhis

- Sayyids founded by Khizer Khan Successors-Mubarak Shah, Muhammad Shah and Alauddin Alam Shah.
- The Lodhis were first Afghans to rule India.
- Bahlol Lodhi (AD 1451-1481) founded the dynasty.
- Sikander Lodhi (AD 1418-1517) introduced Gaz-i-Sikandari. (unit for measuring cultivated filed). He founded Agra in 1504. He wrote the Persian verse 'Gulrukhi'.
- He was succeeded by Ibrahim Lodhi (1517-1526), who was defeated by Rana Sanga of Mewar. He was also defeated by Babur in April, 1526 and let to the establishment of the Mugal rule in India.

PROVINCIAL KINGDOMS

Gujarat

- Broke away from Delhi in AD 1397 under Zafar Khan, who assumed the title fo Sultan Muzaffar Shah.
- His grandson Ahmed Shah I built a new city Ahmedabad.
- The next prominent ruler was Mahmud Beghra. During this rule, the Portuguese set-up a factory at Diu.

Kashmir

- Kashmir was ruled by Hindu rulers until Shamsuddin Shan asserted himself in AD 1339.
- The greatest ruler was Zain-ul-Abidin (AD 1420-70), who is called called the Akbar of Kashmir, built Zaina lake, and artifical islan in Wular lake.

Mewar

- Rajput rule restored by Rana Hamir after Alauddin Khilji captured Chirro in AD 1303.
- The Greatest was Rana Kumha who built the Vijay Stambh at Chittor to commemorate his victor over Muhamad Khalji of Malwa.

Vijayanagara Kingdom

- Founded by Harihara I and Bukka I.
- Devaraya I built a dam across Tungabhara river and Italian traveller Nicolo de Conti visited-his court followed by the Russian merchant Nikitin.
- Devaraya II, who was seen as incarnation of Indra by Commoners; He was also called 'Gajabetekara' and wrote Mahanataka Sudanidhi and commentary on the Brahma Sutras in Sanskrit; Persian Ambassador Abdur Razzq visited his court Krishnadeva Raya (AD 1509-29) was the greatest ruler.
- He was known as Abhinava Bhoja, Andra Pitamah and Andhra Bhoja because of being a great patron of literature.
- Eight great poets of Telugu (Ashta Diggaja) adorned his court like-Pedanna and Tenalirama.
- Portugues Dominigo Paes and Barbosa visited his court.
- Battle of Talikota (AD 1565) Sadasiva, the last ruler of the Tuluva dynasty was defeated by the alliance of Ahmadnagar, Bijapuer, Golconda and Bidar.

Bahmani Kingdom

- Alauddin Hasn bahman Shah (AD 1347-58), also known as Hasan Gangu, founded it with capital Gulbarg.
- Ahmad Shah Wali transferred the capital from Gulbarg to Bidar.
- Bhamani kingdom broke up into :
- Nizamsahis of Ahmadnagar
- Founder Malik Ahmad Bahri
- Adilsahis of Bijapuer
- Founder Yusuf Adil Shah

- Imadsahis of Berar
- Founder Fatullah Khan
- Imau-ul-Mulk
- Qutabsahis of Gloconda
- Founder Quli Qutubj Shah
- Baridsahis of Bidar
- Fonder Ali Barid
- The Gol Gumbaz (a tomb with World's second largest dome) is the mausoleum of Muhammad Adil Shah at Bijapur. It was built by Qutubshah. Gol Gumbaz was completed in AD 1656.
- Muhammad Quli Qutubshah founded Hyderabad and built Charminar.

MUGHAL EMPIRE (AD 1526-1707)

Babur (AD 1526-1530)

- Founder of Mughal empire, who introduced gunpowder in India; defeated Ibrahim Lodhi in the First Battle of Panipat (AD 1526); Rana Sanga (Sangram Singh) at Battle of Khanwa (AD 1527); Medini Rai of Chanderi at Bettle of Chanderi (AD 1528) and Muhmad Lodio at Battle of Ghagra (AD 1529); he wrote Tuzuk-i-Baburi in Turkish language.
- Babur declared Jehad and adopted the title Ghazi.
- Died in 1530 and was buried at Aram Bagh (Agra). Later his body was taken to Bagh-e-Babun (Kabul).

Humayun (AD 1530-1556)

- Built Dinpanah at Delhi as his second capital.
- Sher Shah Suri gradually gained power. He fought two battles with Humayun—Battle of Chausa (AD 1539) and another Battle of Kannauj (AD 1540) culminating into Humayun's defeat.
- Humayun passed 15 years in exile; again invaded India in 1555 with the help of his officer Bairm Khan.
- Died in AD 1556 due to a fall from his library buliding's stairs; Gulbadan Begum, Humayns's half-sister wrote Humayun-nama.

Akbar (AD 1556-1605)

- Coronated at the young age of 14 by Baioram Khan; defeated Hemu at the Second Battle of Panipat (AD 1556) with the help of Bairam Khan; conquered Malwa (AD 1561) defeating Baz Bahadur followed by Garh-Katanga (ruled by Rani Durgawati), Chittor (AD 1568), Ranthambhor and Kalinjar (AD 1569), Gujarat (AD 1572), Mewar (Bettle Haldighati, AD 1576 Akbar and Rana Pratap), Kashmir (AD 1586), Sindh (AD 1593) and Asirgarh (AD 1603).
- Buland Darwaza was constructed at Fatehapur Sikri after victroy over Gujarat in AD 1572.
- Married to Harkha Bai, daughter of Rajput ruler Bharmal.
- Ralph Fitch (in AD 1585) was the first Englishman to visit Akbar's court.
- Abolished Jaziyah (AD 1564); believed in Sulh-i-Kul (peace of all), built Ibadat Khana (Hall of prayer) at Fatehpuer Sikri; issued 'Degree of Infallibility' (AD 1579); formulated religious order Din-i-Ilahi (AD 1582). Birbal was the first to embrace it.
- Land revenue system was called Todar Mal Bandobast or Zabti System measurement of land, classification of land and fixation fo rent; and introduced Mansabdari System (holder of rank) to organise nobility and army.
- The Navratnas included Todar Mal, Abul Fazal, Faizi, Birbal, Tansen, Abdur Rahim Khana-i-Khana, Mullah-do-Pyaza, Raja Man sing and Fakir Aziao-Din.

Jahangir (AD 1605-1627)

- Executed the fifth Sikh guru, Guru Arjun Dev.
- Greatest failure was loss of Kandahar to Persia in AD 1622.
- Married Mehr-un-Nisa in AD 1611 and conferred the title of Nurjahan on her; He established Zanjir-i-Adal at Agra Fort for the seekers of royal justice.
- Captain Hawkins and Sir Thomas Roe visited his court.
- Famous painters in his court-Abdul Hassn, Ustad Mansur and Bishandas.
- Shahjahan (AD 1628-1658)
- Annexed Ahadnagar while Bijapuer and Golconda accepted his overlord-ship.

- Secured Kandahar (AD 1639).
- Two Feanchmen, Bernier and Tavernier and Italian adventurer Manucci visited his court.
- Built Moti Masjid and Taj Mahal at Agra, Jama Masjid and Red Fort at Delhi. His reign considered the Golden Age of the Mughal empire.

Aurangzeb (Alamgir) (AD 1658-1707)

- Aurangzeb became victorious after the brutal war of succession among his brother Dara, Shuja and Murad.
- Rebellions during his rule—Jat Peasantry at Mathura, Satnami Peasantry in Punjab and Bundelas in Bundelkhand.
- the annexation of Marwar in AD 1658 led to a serious rift between Rajput and Mughals after the death of Raja Jaswant Singh.
- Ninthi Sikh Guru, Guru Tegh Bahadur was executed by him in 1675.
- Mughal conquests reached territorial climax during his reign.
- It stretched from Kashmir in North to Jinji in South, from the Hisndukush in West to Chittogong in East.
- He was called Darvesh or a Zinda Pir. He forbade Sati. conquered Gijapur (AD 1686) and Golconda (AD 1687) and reimposed Jaziya in AD 1679.
- He built Biwi ka Makbara on the tomb of his queen Rabaud-Durani at Aurangabad; Moti Masjid within Red Fort, Delhi; and the Jami or Badshahi Mosque at Lahore.

Causes behind the fall of Mughal Empire

- Weak and incompetent successor
- Wars of succession
- Aurangzeb's Deccan, religious and Rajput policies
- Jagirdari crisis
- Growth of Marathas and other regional powers
- Foreign invasions of Nadir Shah (1739) and Abdali.

Sur Dynasty

- The founder of Sur dynasty was Farid.
- Afgan ruler of Bihar, Bahar Kan Lohani gave the title of Sher Shah to Farid. Introduced Silver coin called Rupaya and copper coin Dam.
- Built his tomb at Sasaram and built a new city on the bank of Yamuna river (present dya Purana Qila).

LATER MUGHALS

- Bahadur Shah I (1707-12) Original name was Muazzam; Title-Shah Alam I.
- Jahandar Shah (1712-13) He ascended the throne with the help of Zulfikar Khan; abolished Jizya.
- Farrukhsiyar (1713-19) He lacked the ability and knowledge to rule independently. His reign saw the emergence of the Sayyad Brothers.
- Muhammad Shah (1719-48) Nadir Shah invaded India and took away Peacock throne and Kohinoor diamond.
- Ahmed Shah (1748-54) Ahmed Shah Abdali (General of Nadir Shah) marched towards Delhi and the Mughals ceded Punjab and Multan.
- Alamgir (1754-59) Ahmed Shah occupied Delhi. Later, was plundered by Marathas.
- Shah Alam II (1759-1806) could not enter Delhi for 12 years.
- Akbar II (1806-37) pensioner of East India Company. he gave the title 'Raja' to Rammohan Roy.
- Bahadur Shah II (1837-57) Last Mughal Emperor who was made premier during the 1857 Revolt.

Literature of Mughal Period

Author	Work
Babur	Tuzuk-i-Babari
Abul Fazal	Ain-Akbari, Akbarnamah
Jahangir	Tuzuk-i-Jahangir
Hamid	Padshahnama
Darashikoh	Majn-ul-Bahrain
Mirza Md Qasim	Alomgirnama

MARATHAS (AD 1674-80)

Shivaji (AD 1627-80)

- Born at Shivner to Shahji Bhonsle and Jijabai. His religious teacher was Samarth Ramdas and guardian was Dadaji Kondadev.
- Treaty of Purandar (AD 1665) between Shivaji and Mughals.
- Coronation at Raigarh (AD 1674) adn assumed the title of Haindave Dharmadharak (Protector of Hinduism).
- Ashtapradhan (eight ministers) helped in administration. These were Peshwas, Sar-i-Naubat (Military), Muzamdar or Amaty (Accounts); Waqenavis (Intelligence); Surunavis (Correspondence); Dabir or Sumanta (Ceremonies); Nyayadhish (Justice); and Panditrao (Charity).
- Successors of Shivaji were Shambhaji, Rajaram and Shahu (fought of Bettle of Khed in AD 1708).

Peshwas (AD 1719-18)

- Founded by Balaji vishwanath, who concluded an agreement with the Sayyed Brothers (the king makers in history) by with Mughal emperor Farukh Siyyar recongnised Shahu as the king of Swarajya.
- Baji Rao considered as the "greatest exponent of gureilla tactics after Shivaji"; Maratha power reached its zenith and system of confederacy began; defeated Siddis of Janjira; Conquest of Bassein and Salsette form Portugese.
- Balaji Baji Rao known as Nana Shaib; Third Battle of Panipat (AD 1761) between Marathas and Ahmed Shah Abdail gave a big jolt to the Maratha empire.

MODERN INDIA

Advent of the Europeans

Portuguese

- Vasco-da-Gama reached the port of Calicut in AD 1498 during the reign of king Zamorin. (Hindu ruler of Calicut).
- Settlements Damamn, Salsette, Chaul and Bombay (West coast), San Thome (near Madras) an at Hooghly.
- Alfonso de Albuquerque, the second Governor of India (first being Francisco de Almeida) arrived in AD 1509 and captured Goa in AD 1510.

Dutch

- Dutch East India Company was formed in AD 1602.
- Dutch were def4eated by English at the Bettle of Bedara in AD 1759 and as per agreement, the Dutch gained the control over Indonesia and the British over India, Sri Lanka and Malaya.
- Settlements They set-up their first factory at Masulipatnam in 1605. Their other factories were at Pulicat, Chainsura, Patna, Balasore, Naga-pattanam,j Cochin, Sura, Karikal and Kasimbazar.

English

- The English East India Company was formed in 1599 under a charter granted by Queen Elizabeth in 1600. Jahangir grated a farman to Captain Willian Hawkins permitting the Enlish to erect a factory at Surat (1613).
- In 1615, Sir Thomas Roe succeeded in getting at imperial farman to trade and establish factory in all parts of the Mughal Empire by ruler Jahangir.
- In 1690, a factory was established at Suttanati by Jab Chrnock. In 1698, following the acquisition of zamindari of three villages of Suttanati, Kalikata and Govindpur, the city of Calcutta was founded. Fort William was set-up in 1700.
- In 1717, John Surman obtained a farman from Farrukhsiyar, which gave large concessions to the company. This farman has been called the Magna Carta of the Company.
- Battle of Plassey (1757) English defeated Sirajuddala, the nawab of Bengal.
- Battle of Buxar (1754) Captain Munro defeated joint forces of Mir Qasim (Bengal), Shujauddala (Awadh) and Shah Alam II (Mughal).

Danes

- The Danish East India Company was formed in 1616.

- The Danish colony 'Tranquebar' was established on Southern Coromondel coast of India.
- Settlements Serampur (Bengal) and Tranquebar (Tamil Nadu) sold their settlements to the English in 1845.

French

- The French East India Company was formed by Colbert under state patronage in 1664. The First Franch factory was established at Surat by8 Francois Caron in 1668. A factory at Masulipatnam was set-up in 1669.
- French were defeated by English in Battle of Wandiwash (1760).

Governor-Generals of Bengal

Warren Hastings (AD 1774-85)

- Brought the dual government to an end by the Regulating Act, 1773.
- The Act of 1781 made clear demarcation between the jurisdiction of the Governor General-in-Council and Supreme Court at Calcutta.
- Pitt's India Act (1784), Rohilla War (1774), First Maratha War (1775-1782) and Treaty of Salbai with Marahas (1782) and Second Mysore War (1780-84). Foundation of Asiatic Society of Bengal (1784) in Calcutta by Sir William Jones.
- The translator of Abhigyan- Shakuntalam in English in 1789 and wrote introduction to the English translations go Bhagavad Gita by Charles Wilkins.

Lord Cornwallis (AD 1786-93)

- Third Mysore War (1790-92) and Treaty of Seringapatnam (1792).
- Introduced Permanent Settlement in Bengal and Bihar (1793).
- He is called the Father of Ci vil Services in India, introduced judicial reforms by separating revenue administration from judicial administration and established a system of circles (thanas, headed by a Daraga (an Indian).

Sir Johan Shore (AD 1793-98)

- Played an important role in the introduction of Permanent Settlement.
- Battle of Kharda between the Nizams and the Marathas (1795).

Lord Wellesley (AD 1798-1805)

- Introduction of the Subsidiary Alliance (1798), first alliance with Nizam of Hyderabad followed by Mysore, Tanjore, Awadh, the Peshwa, the Bhonsle and the Scindia.
- Treaty of Bassein (1802) and the Second Maratha War.

George Barlow (1805-07)

- Vellore Mutiny (1806)

Lord Minot I (AD 1807-13)

- Concluded the Treaty of Amritsar with Maharaja Ranjit Singh (1809). Charter Act of 1813 was passed.

Lord Hasting (AD 1813-23)

- Anglo Nepal War (1814-16) are Treaty of Sangauli (1816).
- Third Maraths War (1817-18) dissolution of Maratha confederacy and creation of Bombay Presidency.
- Pindari War and establishment of Ryotwari System by Thomas Munro (1820).

Lord Amherst (AD 1823-28)

- First Burmese War (1824-26), Treaty of Yandaboo (1826) and capture of Bharatpur (1826).

Governor-Generals of India

Lord William Bentinck (AD 1828-35)

- Charter Act of 1833 was passed and he was made the first Governor General of India. Before him, designation given was Governor General of Bengal.
- Carried out social reforms like prohibition of sait (1829) and elimination of thugs (1830). On Macaculay's recommendation, English was made the medium of higher education Suppressed female infanticide and child sacrifice.

Lord Metcalfe (AD 1835-36)

- Known as liberator of the press in India.

Lord Auckland (AD 1836-42)

- First Afghan War (1838-42), a disaster for the English.

Lord Ellenborough (AD 1842-44)

- Brought an end to the Afghan war. War with Gwalior (1843), Annexation of Sind by Charles Napier (1843).

Lord Hardings (AD 1844-48)

- First Anglo-Sikh War (1845-46) and Treaty of Lahore (1846). Gave preference to English educated persons in Employment.

Lord Dalhousie (AD 1848-56)

- Introduction of Doctrine of Lapse and annexation fo Satara (1848), Jaipur and Sambhalpur (1849), Udiapur (1852), Jhansi (1853), Nagpur (1854) and Awadh (annexed in 1856 on account of maladministration).
- Laid down the first railway line between Bombay and Thane (1853), Telegraph line between Calcutta and Agra and Postal reforms (first issue of the Indian stamp in Karachi in 1854) with the Post Office Act.
- Widow Remarriage Act, 1856 (the main force being Ishawer Chand Vidyasagar).
- Started Public Works Department, Grand Trunk Road work and harbour of Karachi, Bombay and Calcutta developed.
- Charter Act, 1853-Selection to Civil Service through Competitive examination.
- Started Engineering College at Roorkee; made Shimla, the summer capital.

VICEROYS OF INDIA

Lord Canning (AD 1856-62)

- The last governor general and the first Viceroy. Withdrew Doctrine of Lapse.
- Revolt of 1857, Mutiny took place. Indian Pnenal Code 1860 was passed.
- Passed the Act, 1858, which ended the rule of the East India Company. The Universities of Calcutta, Bombay and and Madras were established in 1857.

Lord Elgin (AD 1862)

- Wahabi Movement.

Lord Johan Lawrence

(AD 1864-69)

- Established the High Courts at Calcutta, Bombay and Madrash in 1865.
- Telegraphic communication was opened with Europe. created the Indian Forest Department.

Lord Mayo (AD 1869-72)

- Organised the Statistical Survey, of India and for the first time in Indian history, a census was held in 1871.
- Started the process of financial decentralisation in India. Established the Department of Agriculture and Commerce.
- Established the Rajkot College at Kathiawar and Mayo College at Ajmar for the Indian princes.
- He was the only viceroy to be murdered in office by a Pathan convict ln the Andamans in I872.

Lord Northbrooke (AD 1882-76)

- Kuka Rebellion in Punjab, Famine in Bihar.

Lord Lytton (AD 1876-80)

- Known as the 'Viceroy of Reverse Character'.
- Royal Titles Act of 1876 and the assumption of the title of 'Empress of India' by Queen Victoria, the Delhi Durbar in January 1877.
- Vernacular Press Act (also called the 'Gagging Act' to restrain the circulation of printed matter) and the Arms Act (made it mandatory for Indians to acquire license in arms) of 1878.

Lord Ripon (AD 1880-84)

- First Factory Act of 1881 (prohibited labour). Local Self-Government was introduced in 1882.
- Repealed the Vernacular Press Act in 1882. Finances of the centre were divided.
- Lord Ripon is regarded as 'the founding father of local self governance' in India.
- An Education Commission was appointed under Sir William Hunter in 1882 to improve primary and secondary education.
- The Ilbert Bill Controversy (1883) enabled Indian district magistrates to European criminals.

Lord Dufferin (AD 1884-88)

- Third Burmese War (AD 1885-86). Establishment of the Indian National Congress in 1885.

Lord Lansdowne (AD 18s8-94)

- Factory Act of 1891 granted weekly
- holiday and stipulated working hours for women and children.
- Civil services were divided into Imperial, Provincial and Subordinate Services.
- Indian Councils Act of 1892.
- The Durand Commission defined the Durand Line between British India and Afghanistan (now between Pakistan and Afghanistan) in 1893.

Lord Elgin II (AD 1894-99)

- Southern uprisings of 1899. Great famine of 1896-1897 and Lyall Commission on famine was established.

Lord Curzon (AD 1899-1905)

- A Commission was appointed under Sir Thomas Ràleigh in 1902, to suggest reforms regarding universities, the Indian Universities Act of 1904 was passed on the basis of its recommendations.
- Ancient Monuments Preservation Act of 1904. Thus, Archaeological Survey of India was established.
- Agricultural Research Institute was established at Pusa in Delhi. Partitioned Bengal in 1905.

Lord Minto (AD 1905-10)

- Swadeshi Movement (1905-08); foundation of Muslim League (1906); Surat Session and split in the Congress (1907). Morley-Minto Reforms (1909).
- Lord Hardinge (AD 1910-16)
- Capital, shifted from Calcutta to Delhi (1911); Delhi Durbar; Partition of Bengal was cancelled. The Hindu Mahasabha was founded in 1915 by Pandit Madan Mohan Malaviya.

Lord Chelmsford (AD 1916-1921)

- Gandhi returned to India (1915) and founded the Sabarmati Ashram (1916), Champaran Satyagraha, Satyagraha at Ahmedabad, (1981), Kheda Sarlagraha (1918).
- August Declaration (1917) by Montague, the then Secretary of State, and Montford reforms or the Government of India Act of 19119.
- Rowlatt Act (March, 1919) and the Jallianwala Bagh Massacre (13th April, 1919).
- Khilafat Committee was formed and Khilafat Movement started (191 9-20).
- Non-Cooperation Movement started (1920-22). Women's University was founded at Poona (1916).

Lord Reading (AD 1921-26)

- Repeal of Rowaltt Act Chauri-Chaura incident. RSS, founded in 1920. Suppressed Non-Cooperation Movement. Formation of Swaraj Party.
- Moplah Rebellion (1921) took place. Kakori Train Robbery on 1sr August, 1925. Communal Riots of 1923-25 in Multan, Amritsar, Delhi etc.

Lord Irwin (AD 1926-31)

- Simon Commission visited India in 1927, Congress passed the Indian Resolution in 1929.
- Dandi March (12th March, 1930). Civil Disobedience Movement (1 930).
- First Round Table Conference was held in England ln 1930. Gandhi-lrwin Pact.
- Lahore Session of Congress and Poorna Swaraj Declaration (1925).

Lord Willingdon (AD 1931-36)

- Second Round Table Conference in London in 1931 and third in 1932.
- Government of India Act (1935) was passed. Communal Awards (16th August, 1932) assigned seats to different religious communities. Gandhiji went on a epic fast to protest against this division.

Lord Linlithgow (AD 1936-43)

- Congress Ministries resignation celebrated as 'Deliverance Day' by the Muslim League (1939), the Lahore Resolution (23rd March, 1940) of the Muslim League demanding separate state for the Muslims. (It was at this session that Jinnah propounded his Two-Nation Theory). Outbreak of World War II in 1939. Cripps Mission in 1912. Quit India Movement (8rh August, 1942).

Lord Wavell (AD 1943-47)

- Cabinet Mission Plan (16th May, 1946).
- First meeting of the Constituent Assembly was held on 9th December 1946.
- Arranged the Shimla Conference on 25th June, 1945 with the failure of the
- Indian National Congress and Muslim

League.

- Election to the Constituent Assembly were held and an interim government was appointed under Nehru.
- Lord Mount batten

(March to August, 1947)

- Last.Viceroy of British India and the first Governor-General of free India.
- Partition of India decided by the 3rd June Plan or Mountbatten Plan.
- Retired in June, 1948 and was succeeded by C Rajagopalachari, the first and the last Indian Governor- General of Free India.
- Indian Independence Act was passed by the British Parliament on 4th June, 1947, by which India became independent on 15th August, 1947.

THE, REVOLT OF 1857

- Political Causes The policy of Doctrine of Lapsc.
- Economic Causes Heavy taxation evictions, Discriminatory Tariff Po1lcy against Indian products and destruction of traditional handicrafts that hit peasants, artisans and small zamindars.

Causes of Failure

- The Nizam of Hyderabad the Rala of Jodhpur, Scindla cf Gwalior, the Holkar of Indore, the rulers of Patiala, Sindh and Kashmir and the Rana of Nepal provided active support to the British.
- Comparative lack of of efficient leadership.
- Military Discrimination as Indian soldiers were paid low salaries, they could not rise above the rank of subedar and were racially insulted.
- Grievances of Sepays The introduction of Enfield rifle, and its cartridge of which was greased with animal fat, provided the spark.
- British social reforms (widow remarriage, abolition of sati, education for girls, Christian missionaries).

Impact of the Revolt

- The control of Indian administration was passed on to the British Crown by the Government of India Act, 1 858.
- Reorganisation of the army.
- After the revolt, the British pursued the Policy of Divide and Rule.

CHIEF NATIONAL ACTIVITIES

The Indian National Congress

- It was formed in 1885 by AO Hume.
- The first session was held in Bombay under WC bannerjee in 1855 attended by 72 delegates from all over India.
- The firs two decades of INC are described in history as those moderate demands and a sense of confidence in British justice and generosity.
- Moderate leaders Dada Bhai Naoroji, Badruddin Tayabji, Gopal Krishna Gokhale, Surendranath Bannerjje and Anand Mohan Bose.

Partition of Bengal (1905)

- Thc partition wao announced by Lord Curzon on 16th October, 1905 through a royal proclamation, reducing the old province of Bengal in size by creating East Bengal and Assam out the rest of Bengal.

Swadeshi Movement (1905)

- This movement hid its origin in the anti-partition movement of Bengal. Lal, Bal, Pal and Aurobindo Ghosh played an important role INC took the Swadeshi call first at the Banaras Session, 1905 presided over by GK Gokhale.

Muslim League (1906)

- It was set-up in 1906 by Aga Khan, Nawab Salimullah of Dhaka and Nawab Mohsin-ul-Mulk.
- The league supported the Partition of Bengal and opposed the Swadeshi Movement, demanded special safeguards to its community and a separate electorate for Muslims.
- This led to communal differences between the Hindus and the Muslims.

Demand for Swaraj (Calcutta Session in December, 1906)

- The INC, under the leadership of

Dadabhai Naoroji, adopted 'Swaraj' (Self-government) as the goal of Indian people.

Surat Session (1907)

- The INC split into two groups: the Extremists and the Moderates, due to the debate on nature of Swadeshi Movement.
- Extremists were led by Lal, Bal, pal while the Moderates by GK Cokhale.

Morley-Minto Reforms (1909)

- The reforms envisaged a separate electorate for Muslims, besides other constitutional measures.
- Lord Minto came to be known as the fathers of Communal Electorate.

Ghadar Party (1913)

- Formed by Lala Hardayal, Taraknath Das and Sohan Sing Bhakna. Headquarter—Sen Francesco.
- The name was taken from a weekly paper, Ghadar, which had been started on 1st November, 1913 to commemorate the 1857 Revolt.

Home Rule Movement (1916)

- Started by BG Tilak (April, 1916) at Poona and Annie Besant and S Subramania Iyer at Adyar, near Madras (September, 1916).
- Objective Self-government for India in the British Empire.
- Tilak supported the movemnent and joint Annie Besant. He raised the slogan Swaraj is my Birth Right and I shall have it.

Lucknow Pact (1916)

- Pact between INC and Muslim League following a war between Britain and Turkey leading to anti-British feelings among Muslims. Both organisation jointly demand dominion status for the country.

August Declaration (1917)

- After the Lucknow Pact, the British policy was announced which aimed at "increasing association of Indians in every branch of the administration for progressive realisation of responsible government in India as an integral part of the British empire". This came to be called the August Declaration.
- The Montague—Chelmsford reforms or the Act of 1919 was based on this declaration.

Rowlatt Act (18th March, 1919)

- This gave unbridled power to the government to arrest and imprison suspects without trail. This law enabled the government to suspend the right of Habeas Corpus, which had been the foundation civil liberties in Britain.
- Rowlatt Satyagraha was started against the act. This was the first countrywide agitation by Gandhiji.

Jallianwala Bagh Massacre (13th April, 1919)

- People were agitated over the arrest of Dr. Ktchlu and Dr Satyapal on 10th April, 1919.
- General O' Dyer fired at people who assembled in the Jallianwala Bagh, Ameritsar. the Hunter Commission was appointed to enquire into it.
- Rabindra Nath Tagore returned his knighthood in protest.
- Sardar Udham Singh killed General Dayr in Caxton Hall, London.

Khilafat Movement (1920)

- Muslilms were agitated by the treatment done with Tureky by the British in the Treaty that followed the First World War.
- Ali brother, Mohd Ali and Shaukat Ali started this movement. It was jointly led by the Khilafat leaders and the Congress.

Non-Cooperation Movement (1920)

- Congress passed the resolution in its Calcutta Session in September, 1920.
- It was the first mass-based political movement under Gandhiji.
- Resignation from nominated offices and posts in the local bodies.
- Refusal to attend government durbars and boycott of British courts by the lawyers.
- Refusal of general public to offer themselves for military and other government jobs and boycott of foreign goods.

Chauri-Chaura Incident (1922)

- The Congress Session at Allahabad in

December 1921, decided to launch a Civil Disobedience Movement. Gandhiji was appointed its leader. But before it could be launched, a mob of

- People at Chauri-Chaura (near borakhpur) clashed with the police and burnt 22 policemen on 5th February 1922. This compelled Gandhiji to withdraw the Non-Cooperation Movement on 12th February,1922.

Swaraj Patty (1923)

- Motilal Nehru, CR Das and NC Kelkar (called Pro-changers) demanded that the nationalist should end the boycott of the Legislative Councils, enter them and expose them.

Simon Commission (1927)

- It was constituted by John Simon, to review the political situation in India and to introduce further reforms and extension of parliamentary democracy.
- Indian leaders opposed the commission, as there were no Indians in it, they cried Simon Go Back.
- The government used brutal repression and at Lahore, Lala Lajpat Rai was severely beaten in lathi-charge and later succumbed to death.

The Nehru Report (1928)

- After boycotting the Simon Commission, all political parties constituted a committee under the chairmanship of Motilal Nehru and Tej Bahadur Sapru to evolve and determine the principles for the Constitution of India, The report failed.

Lahore Session (1929)

- On 19th December, 1929, under the presidentship of JL Nehru, the INC, at its Lahore Session, declared Poorna Swaraj (complete independence) as its ultimate goal.
- The tri-coloured flag adopted on 31st December, 1929, was unfurled and 26th January, 1930 was fixed as the First Independence Day, to be celebrated every year. Later, this day was chosen as the Republic Day of India.

Dandi March (1930)

- Also called the Salt Satyagraha.
- Gandhiji started his march from Sabarmati Ashram on 12th March, 1930 for the small village Dandi to break the Salt Law.
- He picked a handful of salt and inaugurated the Civil Disobedience Movement.

Civil Disobedience Movement

- Countrywide mass participation by women.
- The Garhwal soldiers refused to fire on the people at Peshalwar.

First Round Table Conference (1931)

- It was the first conference arranged between the British and Indians as equals. It was held on 12th November, 1930 in London to discuss Simon Commission.
- Hindu Mahasabha and Muslim League Participated in it. The conference failed due to absence of the Indian National Congress.

Gandhi Irwin Pact (1931)

- The government represented by Lord Irwin, and INC led by Gandhiji signed a pact on 5th March, 1931.
- In this, the INC called off the Civil Disobedience Movement and agreed to join the Second Round Table Conference.
- The government allowed the villagers on the coast to make salt for consumption and released the political prisoners. The Karachi Session of 1931 endorsed the Gandhi Irwin Pact.

Second Round Table Conference (1931)

- Gandhiji represented the INC and went to London to meet British Prime Minister Ramsay McDonald.
- The conference however failed as Gandhij could not agree with British Prime Minister on his policy of Communal Representation and refusal of the British Government on the basic Indian demand for freedom.

The Communal Award (16th August, 1932)

- Announced by Ramsay McDonald. It showed divide and rule policy of the British.

- It envisaged communal representation of depressed classes, Sikhs and Muslims.
- Gandhiji opposed it, and started fast unto death in Yervada jail.

Poona Pact/Gandhi-Ambedkar Pact (8th September, 1932)

- The idea of separate electorate for the depressed classes was abandoned, but seats reserved for their in the Provincial Legislature were increased.
- Thus, Poona Pact agreed upon a joint electorate for upper and lower castes.

Third Round Table Conference (1932)

- Proved fruitless as most of the national leaders were in prison.

Demand for Pakistan

- In 1930, Iqbal suggested that the North-West provinces and Kashmir should be made Muslim states within the federation,
- Chaudhary Rehmat Ali gave the term Pakistan in 1933.
- Muslim League first passed the proposal of separate Pakistan in its Lahore Session in 1940 (called Jinnah's Two-Nation Theory). It was drafted by Sikandar Hayat Khan, moved by Fazlul Haq and seconded by Khaliquzzamah.
- In December 1943, the Karachi Session of the Muslim League adopted the slogan Divide and Quit.

August Offer (8th August, 1940)

- It offered (i) Dominion status in the unspecified future, (ii) A post-war body to enact the Constitution (iii) To expand the Governor-General's Executive Council to give full weightage to minority opinion.
- This was rejected by the INC, but was accepted by the Muslim League.

The Cripps Mission (1942)

- The British Government with a view to get cooperation from Indians in the Second World War, sent Sir Stafford Cripps to settle terms with Indian leaders.
- He offered dominion status to be granted after war.
- Congress rejected it. Gandhiji termed it as 'a post-dated cheque on a crashing bank'.

The Revolt of 1942 and The Quit India Movement

- Also called the Wardha Proposal, a Leaderless Revolt.
- The resolution was passed on 8t August, 1942 at Bombay Gandhiji gave the slogan Do or Die.
- On 1st August the Congress was banned and its important leaders were arrested. Gandhiji was kept at the Aga Khan Palace, Pune.
- The people became violent. The movement was however, crushed by the government.

Indian National Army (INA)

- Subhash Chandra Bose escaped to Berlin in 1941 and set-up the Indian League there. In July 1943, he joined the INA at Singapore. Ras Bihari Bose handed over the leadership to him.
- INA had three fighting brigades. named alter Gandhi, Azad and Nehru. Rani of Jhansi Brigade was an exclusive women force. INA had its headquarters at Rangoon and Singapore.

The Cabinet Mission Plan (1946)

- Members were Wavell, Patrick Lawrence, Alexander rnd Stafford Cripps.
- Main proposals
  1. Rejection of demand for a full fledged Pakistan.
  2. Loose union under a Centre with Centre's control over defence and foreign affairs.
  3. Provinces were to have full autonomy and residual powers.
  4. Provincial legislatures would elect a Constituent Assembly.
- Both the Congress and the Muslim League accepted it.

Formation of Interim Government (2nd September, 1946)

- It came into existence on 2nd September, 1946 in accordance with Cabinet Mission's proposals and was headed by JL Nehru. Muslim League refused to join it initially

- Prime Minister Attlee on 20th February, 1947 announced that British would withdraw from India by 30th June, 1948.

Formation of Constituent Assembly (December, 1946)

- The Constituent Assembly met on 9th December, 1946 and Dr Rajendra Prasad was elected as its President.

Jinnah's Direct Action Resolution (16th August, 1946)

- The election result did not favour Muslim League, so Jinnah withdrew his acceptance to the Cabinet Mission Plan.
- Muslim League passed a Direct Action Resolution, which condemned both the British Government and the Congress (16th August, 1946). It resulted in heavy Communal riots.
- Jinnah celebrated Pakistan Day on 27th March, 1947.

Mountbatten Plan

(also called 3rd June Plans) (3rd June, 1947)

- The plan formulated by Lord Mountbatten outlined that
- India was to be further divided into India and Pakistan.
- There would be a separate Constitutional
- Assembly for Pakistan to frame its Constitution.
- The princely states would enjoy the liberty, to either join India or Pakistan, or could even remain independent.
- Bengal and Punjab will be partitioned and a referendum in NWFP and Sylhet district of Assam would be held. A separate state of Pakistan would be erected. Boundary Commission was to be headed by Radcliffe.

Partition and Independence (August,1947)

- Indian Independence Act, 1947 implemented on 15th August 1947, abolished the sovereignty of British Parliament. Dominions of India and Pakistan were created. Each dominion was to have a Governor-General, Pakistan was to comprise Sind, British Baluchistan, NWFT, West Punjab and East Bengal.
- Sardar Vallabhbhai Patel, the first Home Minister, integrated all the states by 15th August, 1947. Kashmir Hyderabad, Junagarh, Goa (with Portuguese) and Pondicherry (with French) later acceded to Indian Federation.

Popular Names of Personalities

Popular Name	Personality	Popular Name	Personality
Andhar Kesari	T Prakasam	JP	Jayaprakash Narayan
Babuji	Jagjiwan Ram	Lady with the Lamb	Lala Lajpat Rai
Bapu	Mahatam Gandhi	Line of the Punjab	Napoleon
CR	C Rajagopalachari	Little Corporal	Napoleon
Desh Bandhu	Chitranjan Das	Lokmanya	Bal Gangadhar Tilk
Grand Old man	Dadabhai Naoroji	Jawan	Indian soldier
Lal, Bal, Pal,	Lala Lajpat Rai, Bal Gangadhar Tilak, Bal Gangadhar Tilak, Bipin	Mahamanya	Pandit Madan Mohan Malaviya
	Chandra Pal	Man of Blood	Bismarck
Guru ji	MS Goplvalkar	Netaji	ubhash Chandra Bose

Gurudev	Rabindranath Tagore	Nightigale of India	Sarojini Naidu
Iron man	Vallabhai Patel	Pandit ji	Jawaharlal Nehru
Sparrow	Major Rajender Singh	Shastri Ji	Lal Bahadur Shastri

Newspapers and Journals

Name	Published by
Bengal Gazette	JA Hickey
Kesari	BG Tilak
Maratha	BG Tilak
Amrita Bazar Patrika	Sisir Kumar Ghosh and Motilal Ghosh
Vande Mataram	Aurobindo Ghosh
Bombay Chronicle	Firoz Shah Metha

Books and Authors

Book	Author
Ghulam Giri	Jyotiba Phule
Pather Panchali	B. Bhushan Bannerji
Satyarth Parkash	Sweami Dayanand
Anand Math	Bankim Chandra Chatterji
Unhappy India	Lala Lajpat Rai
India Divided	Rajendra Prasad
The Discovery of India	Jawaharlal Nehru

ART AND CULTURE

Classical Dancers of India

Name	Dancer
Bharatanatyam	Bala Salaswati, CV Chandrasekha, Leeli Simson, Mrinalini Sarabhai, Padma Subramanyam, Rukmini Devi, Sanykuta Panigrahi, Sonal Mansingh, Yamini Krisnamurti.
Kathak	Bharti Gupta, Birju Maharaj, Damayanti Joshi, Durga Das,. Gopi Krishna, Kumudini Lakia, Sumbhu Maharaj, Sisatra Devi
Kuchipudi	Josyula Seethramalah, Vempathi Chinna Satyam
Manipuri	Guru Bipin Sinha, Jhaveri Sisters, Nayana Javeri, Nirmalal Mehta, Savita Mehta

Odissi	Debaprasad Das, Dhirendra nathi Patnaik,j Indran Rahman, Kelucharan Mahapatra, Priyambada Mohanty
Kathakali	Mrinalini Sarabhai, Guru Shankaran, Namboodripad, Thottma Shankaran, Kutti Nayyar, Shankar Kurup, KC Pannikar, TT Ram Kulti
Mohiniattam	Protima Devi, Sanyakra Panigrahi, Sonal Mansingh, Pankaj Charan Das, Kelucharan Mahapatra, Madhvi Mudgal, etc.

State and Folk Dances

Andhra Pradesh	Kuchipucti, Ghantamarclala Oitam Thedal, Veecih Natakarn
Assam	Bihu, Bichhua, Natpuja, Maharas, Kaligopal, Bagurumba, Khel Gopal, Canoe Jhumura Hobtanai
Bihar	Jat-Jatin, Bakho-Bakhain, Panwariya, Sama-Chakwa, Bidesia
Gujarat	Garba, Dandiya Ras, Tippani Juriun, Bhavai
Haryana	Jhumar, Phag, Deph, Dhamla, Loor, Gugga, Khor, Gagor,
Himachal Pradesh	Jhora, Jhali, Chharhi, Dhaman, Chhapeli, Mahasu, Nati, Dangi
Jammu and Kashmir	Rauf, Hikat, Mandjas, Kud Dandi Nach, Damali
Karnataka	Yakshagan, Huttari, Suggi, Kunitha, Karga, Lambi
Kerala	Kathakali (Classical), Ottam thulal, Mohiniattam, Kaikottikali
Maharashtra	Lavani, Nakata, Koli, Lezim, Gafa, Dahikala, Dasavtar or Powada
Odisha	Odissi (Classical), Savari, Ghumara, Painka, Munari, Chhau
Paschim Bangal	Kathi, Gambhir, Dhali, Jatra, Baul, Marasia, Mahal, Keertan
Punjab	Bhangra, Giddha, Daff, Dhaman, Bhand, Naqual
Rajasthan	Ghumar, Chakri, Ganagor, Jhulan Leela, Huma, Suishini, Ghapla, Kabeliya
Tamil Nadu	Bharatanatyam, Kumi, Kolattam, Kavadiss
Uttar Pradesh	Nautanki, Raslila, Kajri, Jhora, Chappeli, Jaita
Uttarakhand	Garhwali, Kumuni, Kajari, Jhora, Raslila, Chappeli

Instruments and Vocalists

Carnatic	MS Subbalakshmi, Balamuralikrishna, Bombay Jaishree, HK Raghavendra, Aryakudi Ramanujan Iyenegar Venkataram, Sitaranam, Mani Krishanswamy, Akhil Krishnan, ML Vasanthakumari, MD Ramanathan, GN Balasubramaniam

Dhrupad	Ussad Rahim Fahim-ud-Dagar, Zahir-ud-din Dagar, Wasif-ud-din Dagar, Bundecha Bandhu, Pt Abhay Narayan Mallick, jPt Ritwik Sanyal, UDay Bawalkar
Hindustani	Shubha Mudal, Madhup, Mukul Sivputra, Pandit Jasraj, Parveen Sultana, Nain Devi, girija Devi, Ustad Gulam Mustafa Khan, Gangubai Hagal, Krshan Hangal, V Rajput, Kumar Gandarva, Faiyyza Kàn Mallikariun Mnasur.
Thumri	Ustad Bade Ghulam Ali Khan, Ustad Mazhar Ali Khan, Ustad Zawad Ali Khan, Prronima Chaudhary,j Shanti Heerananda, Naina Devi Tira Ganguly

Musical Instruments and Instrumentailsts

Istruments		Instrumentalist
Stringed Instruments		
1	Been	Asad Ali Khan, Zia Moin ud-din Khan
2	Santoor	Shiv Kumar Sharma
3	Sarod	Bucldhadev Dasgupia, Ali Akbar Khan, Amlad Ali khan, Bahadur Khan, Sharan Rani, Zarin S Sharma
4	Satang.	Ustad Binda Khan
5	Sitar	Ravi Shankar, Hara Shankar Bhattacharya, NikhiI Banerjee, Vilayat Khan, Mustaq Ali Khan
6	Surb Ahar	Sajjad Hussain, Annapurna
7	Veena	Doraiswamy lyengar, Chittibabu, Emani Sankara Shastri, Dhanammal, S Bala Chandran, KR Kumaraswamy
8	Violin	Gajanan Rao Joshi, MS Gopal Krishnan, TN Krishnan, Baluswarny, Dikshitar Dwaran Venkatasuramy Nardu Lalyuli G Jayaraman, Mysore T Chowdiah, VG Jog
Wind Instruments		
9	Flute	TR Mahalingam, N Ramani, Hari Prasd Chaurasia, Pannalal Ghosh
10	Nadaswaran	Sheikh Chinna Moula, Neeruswamy Pillai, Rajaratanam Pillai
11	Shehnai	Bismilla Khan
Bercussin (Striking Thumping) Instruments		
1·2	Mridangam	Palghat Mani Iyer, Karaikudi R Mani, Palaghat Raghu
13	Pakhawag	Pt Ayodhya Prasad, Gopal Das, Bahu Ram Shanker Pagalads
14	Tabla	Zakir Hussain, NKikil Ghosh, Krioshan Maharaj, All Rakha Khan, Pandit Samta Prasad, Kumar Bose, Lafit Khan
15	Kanjira	Pudukkotai Dakshinamurti Pallai

Culture Institutions

Institutions	Headquarters	Institutions	Headquarters
Anthropological Survey of India, 1945	Kolkata	Sahitya Academy, 1954	New Delhi
		Sangeeta Natak Academy, 1953 New Delhi	
Archaeological Survey of India, 1861	New Delhi	Library of Tibatan Works and Archives	Dharamshala
		Science City	Kolkata
Asiatic Society, 1784 (Sir William Jones)	Kolkata	Vectorial Memorial Hall	Kolkata
Indira Gandhi National Centre for Arts, 1985	New Delhi	Birla Industrial and Tech Museum	Kolkata
Lalit Kala Akademi (National Academy of Fine Arts), 1954	New Delhi	Central Institute of Buddhist Studies	Leh
National Archives of India, 1981	New Delhi	Nava Nalanda Mahavihara	Nalanda (Birla)
National School of Drama, 1959		New Delhi National Gallery of Modern Art	New Delhi

INDIAN ECONOMY

OUTLINE OF INDIAN ECONOMY

- The economy of India is the 6th largest in the world by nominal GDP and 3rd largest by Purchasing Power Pariety (PPP).

Nature of the Indian Economy

(i) Mixed Economy Existence of both public and private sectors. This term was cointed by Pat Mullins and Supported by JM Keyens.

(ii) Agrarian Economy Even after six-decades of independence 58% of the workforce of India is still agriculturist and its contribution of GDP is 17.4% in 2014-15.

Features

- Following are the features of Indian economy (i) Slow growth of national and per capita income. (ii) Capital deficiency and low rate of capital formation, hence low rate of investment, low production, etc; poor quality of human capital. (iii) Over-dependence on agriculture alongwith low productivity in agriculture alongwith low productivity in agriculture; heavy population pressure. (iv) Unequal distribution of income and wealth. (i) Mass poverty, chronic inflation and chronic unemployment.

Issues in Development

- (i) Low per capita income and low rate of economic growth. (ii) High proportion of people below the poverty line. (iii) Imbalance between size, resources and capital. (iv) Problem of unemployment.
- Broad Sectors of Indian Economy
- Primary Sector Agriculture, forestry and fishing.
- Secondary Sector Mining, manufacturing, electricity, gas and water supply and construction.s
- Tertiary Sector (also called service sector) business, transport, telecommunication, banking, insurance, real estate, community and personnel services.

Economic Planning in India

- Planning Commission (1950) was set-up under the Chairmanship of Jawahalal Nehru (Gulzarilla Nanda was the first Deputy Chairman).
- Basic aim of Economic Planning is to bring rapid economic growth through agriculture, industry, power and all other sectors of the economy.

NITI Aoyag

- NITI Aayog or National Institution for transforming India Aayog came into existence on January, 2015; policy-making think-tank of government that replaces Planning Commission and aims to involve states in economic policy making. It will provide strategic and technical advice to the Central and the State Governments.
- The Prime Minister heads the Aayog as its chairperson. Avrind Panagariya is the Vice-chairperson of NITI Aayog of India.

Historical Milestones

- Planned Economy for India (1934) M Vivesvaraya
- National Planning Committee (1938) Jawaharlal Nehru.
- Bombay Plan (1944)
- Gandhian Plan (1944) SN Agarwal
- People's Plan (1945) MN Roy
- Sarvodaya Plan (1950) JP Narayan

Five Year Plans At a Glance

Plan	Growth Rate		Important Sector
	Target	Achieve	
First Plan (1951-56) (Based on Harrod Domar Model)	2.1%	3.6%	Agriculture, irrigation, electricity
Second Plan (1956-61) (Based on PC Mahalanobis Tow sector model)	4.5%	4.2%	Heavy industries
Third Plan (191-66) Plan Holiday (1966-69)	5.6%	2.8%	Foodgrains, heavy industries
Fourth Plan (1969-74)	5.7%	3.3%	Agriculture
Fifth Plan (1974-78)	4.4%	4.8%	Rolling Plan (1978-80)
Sixth Plan (1980-85)	5.2%	5.4%	Agriculture, industries
Seventh Plan (1985-90)	5.0%	6.0%	Energy foodgrains
Two Annual Plan (1990-92) Eight Plan (1992-97)	5.6%	6.6%	Human resource education
Ninth Plan (1997-2002)	6.5%	5.4%	Social justice
Tenth Plan (2002-07)	8.1%	7.5%	Income, energy
Eleventh Plan (2007-2012)	8.0%	7.9%	Inclusive growth
Twelfth Plan (2012-2017)	8%	—	Faster, sustainable and more inclusive growth

Human Development Index (HDI)

- HDI measures the average achievements in a country in three basic dimensions of the human development; a long and healthy life, access to knowledge and a decent standard of living.
- The United National Development Programme (UNDP) introduced the HDI in its first Human Development Report (HDR) preparedj under the stewardship of Mahbub-ul-Haq in 1990. In the HDR 2016, India has been ranked 131 out of 188 countries in term of HDI.

National Income of India

- National Income (NI) is the net value of all the final goods and services produced by its nationalas during a financial year. In India, the financial year is form 1st April to 31st March. The National Income is calculated annually.
- When NNP is calculated at Factor Cost (FC) it is called National Income. This measure is calculated by deducting indirect taxes and adding subsidies in NNP at Market Price (MP).
- Gross Domestic Product (GDP) is the total money value of all final goods and services produced within the geographical boundaries of the country during a given period of time.
- When the National Income is measured at the base year price, it is called National Income at constant price.
- When the National Income is measured at the base year price, it is called National Income at constant price.
- Depreciation is substance from GDP and net factor income from abroad is added to get net national product at market price.
- Gross Value Added (GVA) is measure of the value of goods and services produced in an area, industry or sector of an

economy. In national accounts, GVA is output minus intermediate consumption.

Indian Tax Structure

- Direct Tax The term direct tax generally means a tax paid directly to the government by the persons on whom it is imposed. e.g. income tax, Corporate income tax, capital gain tax, stamp duty, land tax, estate duty, wealth tax, petroleum revenue tax. The government earns maximum from corporate income tax.
- Indirect Tax An indirect tax is a tax collected by an intermediary from the person who bears the ultimate economic burden of the tax. e.g. sales tax or VAT, customs duty, insurance premium tax, excise duties, landfill tax, electricity duty, climate change levy.

Goods and Service Tax (GST)

- Goods and Services Tex (GST) came into force from July 1, 2017.
- The GST as it is more commonly referred to is a system of taxation where there is a single tax in the economy for goods as well as services. Indian GST was first proposed in India in the Union Budget speech in 2006-07.
- The main feature of the GST is that there is a tax credit available at each stage of the value chain.

Inclusive Development

Human Development Index (HDI)

- HDI measure was given by Pakistani Nabel Prize Winner, Mehbub-ul-Haq.
- Level of Human development is measured by Human Development Index (HDI), published by UNDP since, 1990.
- Three dimensions
  1. Life expectancy at birth rate;
  2. Education Index comprising means year of schooling and expected year of schooling;
  3. GNI per capita (PPP US $) Index.

Programmes/Measures

- NRHM (National Rural Health Mission) was launched on 2nd April, 2005 to reduce IMR and MMR.
- NUHM (National Urban Health Mission) launched on 2013. Education programmes like Shiksha Abhiyan, Mid-Day Meal Scheme etc.
- Rurla development programmes like MENREGA and Bharat Nirman.

Inequality

- According to HDR-2011, inequality in India for the period 2000-2011 in terms of the income Gini coefficient was 36.8, which is the most favourable among the BRICS countries.

Programmes/Measures

- Adoption of progressive taxation in India. Anti-poverty and employment generation programmes.
- Land reforms like abolition of intermediaries, land ceiling acts tenancy reforms and co-operative movement were launched.
- Rural Development Programmes.
- Backward region grant fund.

POVERTY

- The erstwhile Planning Commission estimated poverty rate based on data collected by National Sample Survey Organisation (NSSO).
- Main Reasons for Rural Poverty Rapid population growth, lack of capital, lack of alternate employment other than poor agriculture, illiteracy and lack of proper implementation of PDS.
- Main Reasons for Urban Poverty Migration for rural areas, lack or skilled labour, lack of housing facilities, limited job opportunities in cities.
- Based on 2400 calories (rural) and 2100 calories (urban) and monthly per capita consumption expenditure of (rural) Rs. 540 (urban), Planning Commission (Now NITI Aagyog) estimated poverty ratio in India in 2004-05 was 27.5% and according to the Suresh Tendulkar Committee was 37.2%.
- The Tendulkar Committee stipulated a benchmark of daily per capita expenditure of and rural and urban areas, respectively.

Socio-Economic Programmes

Programme/Measure	Year of Launch
Drought Prone Area Programme	1973-74
Twenty Point programme	1975
Integrated Rural Development Programee	1980
Indira Awaas Yojana	1985
Jawahar Rozgar Yojana	1989
Nehru Rozgar Yojana	1989
Swarna Jayanti Shahri Rozgar Yojana	1997
Pradhan Mantri Gramodaya Yojana	2000
Pradhan mantri Gram Sadak Yojana	2000
Sampoorna Grameen Rozgar Yojana	2001
Bharat Nirman	2005
Jawaharlal Nehru National Urban Renewal Mission	2005
Prime Minister Employment Generation Programme	2008
Mahatma Gandhi National Rural Employment Programme	2009
National Rural Livelihood Mission (NRLM)	2011
Nirmal Bharat Abhiyan	2012
Swachh Bharat Abhiyan	2014
Shyama Prasad Mukherji Urban Mission	2014
Beti Bachao Beti Badhao	2014
Pradhan Mantri Jan Dhan Yojana	2015
Atal Pension Yojana	2015
Deen Dayal Upadhyay Gram Jyoti Yojana	2015
Digital India Programme	215
National Skill Development Mission	2015
HRIDAY (Heritage City Dvelopment and Augmentation Yojana)	2015
Smart City Mission	2015
Atal Mission for Rejuvenation and Urban Transformation	2015
Pradhanmantri Suraksha Beema Yojana	2015
Shyama Prasad Mukherji Rurban Mission	2015
Pradhan Mantri Krishi Sinchayee Yojana	2015
Start-up and Stand-up Yojana	2015
Pradhan Mantri Fasal Bima Yojana	2015
Pradhan Mantri Ujjwala Yojana	2016
SWAYAM (Study Webs of Active-Learning for Young Aspiring Minds)	2015
Pradhan Mantri Garib Kalyan Yojana	2016
Ayushman Bharat health insurance	2018

EMPLOYMENT

- A person, working 8 hours a day for 273 days of the year is regarded as employed as the main worker.

Est mates Causes

- Since 1973 on the recommendation of B Bhawati Committee, three estimates o unemployment have been brought about by Planning Commission, viz
  1. Usual Principal Status Persons who remained unemployed for a major part of the year.
  2. Current Weekly Status Person who did not find even an hour of work during the survey week.
  3. Current Daily Status Persons who did not find work on a day or some days during the survey week.

Women Empowerment and Child Development

Programme/Measure	Year
Mid-Day Meal Scheme	1995
Swadhar	1998
Swayam Sidha	2001
SSA	2001

Support to Training and Employment Programme for Women (STEP)	2003-04
Ujjwala	2007
Dhanlaxmi	2008
Integrated Child Protection Scheme	2009-10
Sabla Scheme	2010
National Mission for Empowerment of Women	2010
Bal Bandu Scheme	2011

AGRICULTURE

- Agriculture is the mainstay of Indian economy. It makes important contribution in GDP, National Income, employment, trade and industry.
- Green Revolution si associated with the use of HTVS (High Yielding Variety Seeds), chemical, fertiliser and new technology, which led to a revolutionary results in agricultural production.
- The term 'Green Revolution' was given by American Scientist Dr William Gaud.

Major Agricultural Revolutions

Revolution	Production
Blue	Fish Production
Golden Fiber	Jute
Pink	Onion
Red	Meat
White	Milk
Yellow	Oilseed

Tricolour revolutions

Tricolour revolution has 3 components

- Saffron revolution-Solar energy
- White revolution-Cattle welfare
- Blue revolution-fisherman's welfare

INDUSTRIES

Industrial Policies

- Industrial polices were launched in 1948, 1956, 1977, 1980 and 1991.
- Industrial Policy 1956 is called Economci Constitution of India and gave public sector the strategic edge.
- Industrial Policy 1991 opened up the economy. Its main aims were
  - (a) to end license-permit raj;
  - (b) to integrate Indian economy with the outer world;
  - (c) to remove restrictions on FDI and
  - (d) to reform public sectors.

Public Sector Enterprises (PSEs)

- Industries requiring compulsory licensing (a) distillation and brewing of alcoholic drinks; (b) cigar and cigarettes fo tobacco; (c) electronic aerospace and defence equipment; (d) industrial explosives; (e) specific hazardous chemicals.
- Areas reserved for public sector are (a) atomic energy—production separation and enrichment of fissionable materials and (b) railways.
- Present Policy on PSEs is to (a) not to privatise profit-making companies and to modernise and revive sick companies; (b) not to bring government stake in PSEs below 51%; (c) to adopt initial public offering rute to disinvestment.
- There are 298 central PSEs as on 31st March, 2015.

Maharatnas, Navratnas, and Miniratnas

- To impart greater managerial and commercial autonomy the PSEs the comcept of Maharatna, navratna and Miniratna was started.
- Maharatnas were started in 2009. Seven Maharatnas are ONGC, SAIL, IOC, NTPC, Coal India Ltd, BHEL and GAIL (India) Ltd.
- Navratnas Bharat Electronics Ltd, BPCL, HAL, HPCL, MTNL< NALCO, National Mineral Development Corporation, Nevyeli Lignite Company Ltd, Power Grid Corporation of India Ltd, Rashtriya Ispat Nigma Ltd, Rural Electrification Corporation Ltd, Rural Electrification Corporation Ltd, Shipping Corporation of India Ltd, CCIL, EIL and NBCCL.
- Miniratnas Public Sector Enterprises (PSEs) that have made profit

continuously for the last three years or earned a net profit of crores or more in one the three years.

- At present there are 56 in category I and 17 in Category. II. NEEPCO is newly added miniratna in category I.

Industrial Committees

- Hazari Committee on Industrial Policy.
- Subimal Dutt Committee on Small Scale Industry.
- Abid Hussain Committee on Small Scale Industry.
- C Rangarajan Committee on disinvestment.
- Memorandum of Understandings (MoU) Arjun Sengupta.

Small Scale Industry

- A new thrust to Small Scale Industry, given in Industrial Policy of 1977.
- MSMED Act, was enacted in 2006.
- Contributes 8% to GDP, 45% to all manufactures and 42% to exports.
- According to the 4th census (2009) of SSIs, 67% of the MSME are in manufacturing and 33% are in services sector.

Major Industries in India

Iron and Steel

- First Steel Industry at Kalti, Wast Bengal—Bengal Iron Works company was established in 1874.
- First large scale steel plant—TISCO at Jamshedpur (1907) was followed by IISCO at Burnpur (1919), West Bengal.
- The first public owned steel plant was Rourkela integrated steel plant. presently, India is the 3td largest producer of steel and comes 1st in the production of sponge iron.

Location (Plants)	Assistance
Rourkela (Odisha)	Germany
Bhilai (Chhattisgarh)	Russia
Durpapur (West Bengal)	Britain
Bokaro (Jharkhand)	Russia
Viskhapatnam (Andhra Pradesh)	Russia

Sugar Industry

India is the second largest producer of sugar in the world with a 22% share. It is the second largest agro-based industry in the country.

Jute Industry

- India ranks no 1 in jute production and no 2 in raw jute export after Bangladesh.
- More than two third jute industry in concentrated in West Bengal.

Cotton and Textile Industry

- Largest organised and broad-based industry accounting for 4% of GDP, 20% of manufacture value added and one third of total exports earning.

Cement Industry

- First cement producing unit was set-up at West Bengal, Porbandar (Gujarat) in 1914.
- India is the second largest producer of cement in the world.

Committees on Various Sectors of Indian Economy

AC Shah Committee	Non-Banking Financial Company
Bimal Jalan Committee	Market Infrastructure Instruments
Malegam Committee	Functioning of Micro Finance Institutions
Birla Committee	Corporate Governance
Kirit Parikh Committee	Rationalisation fo Petroleum Product Prices
Chaturvedi Committee	Improving National Highways in India
SR Hashim Committee	Urban Poverty

Abhiji Sen Wholesale	Price Index
C Rangarajan	Services Price Index
Abid Hussain Committee	Development of Capital Markets
Damodaran Committee	Customer Service in Banks
Khandelweal Committee	Human Resource in Commercial Banks
Patil Committee	Corporate Debt
VK Sharma Committee	Credit to Marginal Farmers
Sarangi Committee	Non-Performing Assets
Khanna Committee	Regional Rural Banks
Dantawala Committee	Lead Bank Scheme
Gadgil Committee	Financial Inclusion

BANKING AND FINANCE

- Bank of Hindustan was the first bank, established in India in 1770.
- First bank with limited liability managed by an Indian Board was the Oudh Commercial Bank in 1881.
- First purely Indian bank was Punjab National Bank (1894).

Nationalisation of Bank

- A step toward social banking was taken with the nationaslisation of 14 commercial banks on July 19, 1969. Six more banks were nationalsied on 1980, total number of public sector banks are 27.
- Later on, in the year 1993, the government merged New Bank of India with Punjab National Bank.
- Alies of State Bank of India merged with SBI on April 1, 2017. Bhartiya Mahila Bank (BMP) also merged in SBI.
- IDBI Bank is an Indian financial service company, formerly known as Industries Development Bank of India, headquartered in Mumbai, India.
- In September, 2004, the RBI incorporated IDBI as a scheduled bank under the RBI Act, 1934.
- UDaya Kumar Dharmalingam is the designer of the Indian rupee sign .

Reserve Bank of India (RBI)

- RBI was established in 1935, under RBI Act, 1934. RBI is the Central Bank of India. The main purpose of creating RBI was to separate currency and credit from Government of India. RBI was nationalised in 1949 and its first Indian Governor was CD Deshmukh. Its headquarter is in Mumbai.

New Bank Licence

- In April 2015, Reserve Bank of India Provided licence for operation to two new private banks namely bandhan Financial Services and Infrastructure Development Finance Company (IDFC).

MUDURA Bank

- Micro Units Development and Refinance Agency Bank (MUDRA Bank) was launched on 8th April, 2015. Bank ast up under SIDBI (Small Industries Development Bank of India). Bank has launched 3 loan instruments.
- Shishu-Cover loans upto Rs. 50,000
- Kishore-Cover loan above Rs. 50,000 and upto 5 lakh.
- Tarun-Cover loans above 5 lakh and upto 10 lakh

The RBI and Credit Control Quantitative Credit Control

It is used to control the volume of credit and indirectly to control the inflationary and deflationary pressures. The quantitative credit control consists of

- Repo Rate It is the rate, at which RBI lends short-term money to the banks against securities. Repo rate injects liquidity in the market.

- Reverse Repo Rate It is the rate, at which banks part short-term excess liquidity with the RBI. This is always 100 base point, 1% less than Repo rate.
- Bank Rate is the rat, at which the RBI gives finance to Commercial banks.
- Cash Reserve Ratio (CRR) Cash that banks deposits with the RBI without any floor rate or ceiling rate.
- Statutory Liquidity Ratio (SLR) It is the ratio of liquid asset, which all Commercial Banks have to keep is the from of the cash, gold and unencumbered approved securities equal to not more than 40% of their total demand and time deposits liabilities (ranges is 25-40%).

Qualitative/Selective/Direct Credit Control

Qualitative measure are used to make sure that purpose, for which loan is given is not misused. it is done through

- credit rationing
- regulating loan to consumption etc

Functions of the RBI

- Monetary policy, regulation and supervision of the banking and non-banking finance institutions.
- Debt and cash management for Centre and State Governments.
- Foreign exchange management, current and capital account management.
- Management of foreign exchange reserves.
- Currency management; oversight of the payment and settlement systems.
- Development role.
- Research and statistics.

Indradhanush Scheme 2015

- This is for the banking reforms in India. The 7 key reforms of Indradhanush Mission include, appointments de-stressing, capitalisation, empowerment, framework of accountability, governance reforms and bank board bureau.

14th Finance Commission

- The 14th Finance Commission was constituted in accordance with the Articles 270, 275 and 280 of the Indian Constitution.
- The first finance commission was headed by KC Neogi and the 14th Finance Commission is headed by Yaga Venugaopal Reddy.

Stock Exchange of India

- Capital market is the market for long-terms funds while money market is the market for short-term funds.
- Capital market of India is regulated by SEBI (Securities and Exchange Board of India 1988).
- A Stock Exchange provides services for brokers and traders to trade stocks, bonds and other securities.
- The Bombay Stock Exchange (BSE) is a stock exchange located on Dalla Street, Mumbai and is the oldest stock exchange in Asia. The BSE has the largest number of listed companies in the world established in 1875.
- The National Stock Exchange (NSE) is the 16th largest stock exchange in the world. jIt is situated in Mumbai.

Insurance

- Insurance industry8 includes two sector life Insurance and Central Insurance.
- LIC was established on September 1, 1956.
- Insurance Regulatory and Development Authority of India (IRDAI) was set-up on 19th April, 2000. Protect and regulate by Insurance Sector by IRDA has changed its name to insurance Regulatory and Development Authority of India in December 2014.

Foreign Trade

Balance of Trade (BoT)

- The difference between a nation's imports of goods and services and its exports of them is known as Balance of Trade. There are three possibilities in the Balance of Trade (BoT) which are as follows
  1. Balance BoT i.e. Exports Imports
  2. Adverse BoT i.e. Exports Imports
  3. Eavourable BoT Export > Imports

Balance of Payment (BoP)

- BoP records the transactions in goods, services and assets between residents of a country with the rest of the world for a specified time period typically a years.

There are two amin accounts in the BoP : the current account and the capital account. In addition to that BoP includes errors and omissions and change in foreign exchange reserves.

Foreign Direct Investment (FDI)

- It is an investment in a foreign country through the acquisition of a local company or the establishment of an operation on a new Greenfield site. Direct investment implies control and managerial and perhaps technical, input.

FDI Limits

Census	% of FDI/ Equity
Multi Brand Retail (food)	100%
Telecom Services	100%
Tea Plantation	100%
Asset Reconstruction Company	100%
Petroleum and Natural Gas	49%
Commodity Exchanges, Insurance	49%
Power Exchanges	49%
Stock Exchanges/ Clearing Corporations	74%
Credit information Companies	74%
Courier Services	100%
Single Brand Product Retail Trading	100%
Defence Sector	100%

CENSUS 2011

Population	Trend in India	Total Population	1210569573
1891-1921	Stagnant population	Male	523121843 (51.47%)
1921-1951	Steady growth	Female	587447730 (48.53%)
1951-1981	Rapid high growth (stage of population explosion)	Density	382 per sq km
		Sex Ratio	943
1981-2001	High growth rate with definite sings of slowing down	Child Sex Ratio	914

Largest and the Smallest States/UTs (in Population)

Top States/UTs		Bottom States/UTs	
Uttar Pradesh	199281477	Lakshadweep	64429
Maharashtra	112372972	Daman and Diu	242911
Bihar	103804637	Dadra and Nagar Haveli	342853
West Bengal	91347736	Andaman and Nicorbar Islands	379944
Andhra Pradesh	84665533	Sikkim	607688

Effective Literacy Rate
(2001-2011)

	2001(%)	2011(%)	Difference
Persons	64.83	74.04	10.21
Fenakes	56.67	65.46	118.8

States/UTs (according to Literacy)

Top States/UTs	(in %)	Bottom States/UTs	(in %)
Kerala	93.91	Bihar	63.82
Lakshadweep	92.28	Arunachal Pradesh	66.95
Mizoram	91.58	Rajasthan	67.06
Tripura	87.75	Jharkhand	67.63
Goa	87.40	Andhra Pradesh	67.66

Sex Ratio

	2011		2011	
	Population (in mn)	**Population (in mn)**	**Population (in mn)**	**Population (in mn)**
Males	532.2	51.74	623.7	51.51
Female	496.5	48.26	586.4	48.46
Adult Sex Ratlon	**933**		**943**	
				943
Males	85.0	51.89	82.9	52.24
Females	78.6	48.11	75.8	47.76
Child Sex Ratio	**927**		**914**	

GENERAL SCIENCE

BIOLOGY

- Biology (coined by Lamarck and Treviranus 1802), is a branch of science which deals with study of living organisms. It mainly includes botany (Study of plants) and Zoology (Study of animals).

Living World

- Carolus Linnaeus developed binomial nomenclature for living organisms In 18th Century , scientific name consisting of genus and species.
- Whittaker (1969) classified living organisms into five kingdoms—Monera, Protista, Fungi, Plantae and Animalia.
- Monera includes bacteria and Mycoplasma, while Protista includes Protozoa (unicellular Eukaryotes).
- Viruses are sub-microscopic, obligate, intracellular parasite consisting of nucleoprotein.
- WM Stanely firstly crystallised TMV (Tobacco Mosaic Virus).
- Viroids are smallest infectious single stranded RNA molecules discovered by TO Diener.

The Cell

- According to cell theory proposed by Schleiden and Schwann (1838) cell is the structural and functional unit of living organisms.
- An organism may be composed of single cell (unicellular) or may cells (multicellular).
- Cells are two types , prokaryotic (which lacks nucleus and membrane bound organelles) and eukaryotic (which have nucleus and membranes bound organelles.)
- Prokaryotic cell is found in bacteria, mycoplasma and blue-green while eukaryotic cell in plants, animals and fungi.

Nucleic Acids

- These contain the genetic instructions used in the development and functioning of all known living organisms. These are of two types namely DNA and RNA.
- Deoxyribo Nucleic Acid (DNA). It is a long polymer made from repeating units called nucletiodes. It has four bases i.e. adenine, guanine, cytosine and thymine.
- Rib Nucleic Acid (RNA) It is also made up of a long chain of nucleotides. It contains uracil in place of thymine.

Human System

- The cells of human and other multicellular animals are organised into tissues. Two or more tissues groped together to form organs. An organ system is a group of organs that function together to carry out the principal activities of the body.

Digestion

- Digestion is the process by which complex food in converted into simple components with the help of digestive enzymes, hydrolysis process.

Respiratory System

- Respiration in an oxidative process involving oxidation of food substances such as carbohydrate,j fat and proteins to form , water and to releases energy.
- Respiration may be anaerobic, (without) and aerobic (with O).

Respiratory Organs of Animals

Organ	Animal
Lungs	Reptiles and Mammals
Skin	Frog, earthworm and leeches

Gills	Fishes, tadpoles and prawns
Tracheae	ncests, centipedes and millepedes
Body surface	Protozoans, Porifera and coelenterates
Book lungs	Spider and scorpion
Book gills	King crab, pawn, cray fish and Daphnia
Mental	Mollusca (Unio)
Air bladdar	Long fish and bony fishes (e.g. Labeo)
Airsacsllungs	Birds

Blood (Lymphatic System)

- Fluid connective tissue composed of plasma and blood cells.
- An adult person had 5-6 litre blood.
- It is slightly alkaline having pH 7.3-7.4.
- Plasma is pale yellow transparent and constitute about 60% volume of blood.
- Plasma is composed of 90-92% water, 7% organic substances (albumin, globulin and fibrinogen protein) and 1% inorganic substance.
- Neutorphils (65%) are phagocytic granulocyte and increase during bacterial infection.
- Red blood corpuscle (Most abundant) are non-nucleated and contains hemoglobin (the respiratory pigment).
- white blood cells are colourless, nucleated and granular or a granular.
- Eosinophils are also called acidophils (2-8%) are phagocytic granulocyte and play important role in hypersensitivity.
- Basophils (2%) are non-phagocytic granulocyte and increases during chickenpox. .

Blood Groups, Genotypes and their Transfusion Possibility

Blood Groups (phenotype)	Antigen in Red Blood Cells	Antibodies in Plasma	Can Give Blood to Groups	Can Receive Blood from Group
O	None	Anti-, Anti-	O, A, B and AB	O
A	A	Anti-	A and AB	O and A′
B	B	Anti-	B and AB	O and B
AB	A and B	None	AB	O, A, B and AB

- Monocytes (0.5%) are agranulocytes called policeman of blood and increase during tuberculosis.
- Lymhocytes (26%) are agrnucolcytes producing antibodies and increase during viral infection.
- Platelets (thrombocytes) are non-nucleated. Platelets have a life span of about 8 to 10 days.
- Rh factor discovered by Landsteiner and Veiner in Rhesus monkey, which is responsible for erythoroblastosis foetalis disease.
- Important component of blood clotting are fibrinogen, prothrombin, thromboplastin, calcium ions and Vitamin-K.

Heart

- Human heart is myogenic contraction is initiated by a pulse produced by Sinu Atrial node (SA node) locatedj in right atrium. It is also called pacemaker. First heart sound is lub and second heart sound is dub.
- Contraction of heart is called systole. 120 mm Hg, while relaxation is called diastole (80 mm Hg).

Excretion

- It is the process elimination of harmful waste products from the animal body to regulate the composition of body fluids and tissues.

- Human excretory system is composed of two kidneys. Nephron is the structural and functional unit of kidneys.
- Colour of urine is ale yellow. It is due to pigment urochrome.
- Human urine contains about 95% water, 2% salts, 2.6% urea and 0.3% uric acid.

Main Excretory Organs

Excretor Organ	Animal
Contractive vacuole	Amoeba
Flame cells/ solenocytes	Tapeworm
Renette cell	Ascaris
Nephridia	Earthworm
Malpighian tubules	Cockroach
Coxal glands	Scorpion
Green glands	Prawn

- pH of urine is about 6.0 (mildly acidic).
- The urine on standing given a pungent smell. It is due to the conversion of urea into ammonia.
- Specific gravity of urine is 1.015-1.025.
- Volume of urine is 1 to 2 L per day.

Main Excretory Products

Product	Animal
Ammonia	Most invertebrates, fishes etc
Urea	Ascaris, earthworm, cartilaginous fishes, amphibian and mammals
Uric acid	Insects, land reptiles and birds

Central Nervous System

- The brain is the organising and processing centre of the body. It is the site of consciousness, sensation, memory and intelligence.
- The brain receives impulses from the spinal cord and from 12 pairs of cranial nerves coming from it and extending to the senses and to other organs. In addition, the brain initiates activities without environmental stimuli.
- Three major portions of the brain are3 recognised as the hindbrain, midbrain and the forebrain.

Important Functions of Brain

Forebrain

Olfactory region	Smell
Cerebrum	Thinking, intelligence, memory, ability to learn from experience, will power, skilled work, reasoning knowledge, consciousness and speech.
Control	Laughing, weeping, micturition (passing of urine), defecation voluntary forced breathing and voluntary muscular co-ordination.
Diencephalon (sensation of)	Heat, cold and pain control centre of autonomic nervous system, control hunger, thirst, sweating, sleeping and sex.
Hypothalamus	Regulated body temperature so 'thermostat' of body. Appetite and safety control emotions like love, anger, pleasure and satisfaction. Control metabolism of carbohydrate, fat and water.
Midbrain and Hindbrain	Reflex centre of visual and auditory sensation.

Cerebellum	Involuntary muscular co-ordination, maintain posture, orientation and equilibrium of the body.
Medulla oblongata	Regulate heart rate, involuntary breathing, respiratory centre, blood pressure, (vasoconstriction and vasodilation) gut peristalsis, food swallowing and vomiting gland secretion.

Human Diseases Caused by Fungi

Disease	Fungus
Aspergillosis	Aspergillus flavus, A funigatus and A niger
Blastomycosis	Blastomyces dermatitidis
Candidiasis	Canadida albicans
Chromomycosis	Cladosporium corrionii
Coccodiomycosis	Coccodiodes immities
Cryptococcosis	Lipomyces neoformans
Geotrichosis	Geotrichum candidum
Histroplasmosis	Histoplasma capsulatum
Neuritis	Mucor pusillus
Onychomycosis	Trichophyton purpurenum

Animal/Human Diseases Caused by Fungi

Disease	Fungus
Athlete foot	Trichophyton
Ringworm	Trichopyton, Microsporum and Epidemrophyton
Mucormycosis	Mucor and Rizopus
Penicilliosis	Penicillum

Important Vaccines Discoverer

Vaccine	Discovered By
Small pox	Edward Jenner (1786)
Cholera	Louis Pasture (1880)
Diphtheria and Tetanus	Emil Adolf Von Behring and Shibasabura Kitasato
Tuberculosis	Leaon Calmette and Camille Guerin (1992)
Polio	Jonas E Salk (1954)
Oral polio	Albert Bruce Sabin (1954)
Measles	John F Enders (1960)
Rabies	Charles Nicolle (1909)

Some Antibiotics Developed through Biotechnology

Antibiotic	Microbial Source
Penicillin	Penicillium notatum and P chrysopgenum
Bacitracin	Bacillus subtilis
Cephalosporin	Cephalosporium acremonium
Griseofulvin	Penicillium griseofulvum
Streptomycin	Steptomyces griseus
Tetracycline	S erythraeus
Erythromycin	S aureofaciens
Chloramphenicol	S venezuelae

Ebola Virus

According to World Health Organisation WHO's 19th August, 2015 Situation Report, there were three confirmed cases of Ebola reported int eh week up to 16th August all of which were reported from Guinea. For the first time since the beginning of the outbreak in Sierra Leone, a full epidemiological week has passed with no confirmed cases reported. A total of 72 cases remain under monitoring in Sierra Leone.

On 29th, June 2015, a confirmed case of Ebola was reported in a 17 year old male who had died in Liberia.

Apart from Africa, ebola virus has spread to USA, Spain, Mali and to an extent in Italy and UK.

ECOLOGY

- **Ecology** (term used by Reiter) deals with various principles which govern the relationship between organisms and their environment. Pyramid of number is upright isn grassland and pond ecosystem, while inverted in tree ecosystem.
- Pyramid of biomass is upright in grassland and forest ecosystem where as, inverted in pond ecosystem.
- Pyramid of energy is always upright.

Pollution

- Motor vehicle contribute 60% of air pollution in major cities. Photochemical smog comprising of , HO, PAN, etc.
- CO has 250 times more binding affinity with haemoglobin as compared to O.
- Acid rain is composed of HSO and HNO.
- Chlorofluorocarbons released into stratosphere release free chlorine atom that causes depletion of ozone.
- Sewage is major source of water pollution.
- Bioremediation is the process of using micrp-organisms to remove environmental pollutant, e.g., using oil-zapper developed by TERI to prevent oil spills.
- **Biomagnificaion** The increase in concentration of persistent chemicals in organismas in successive trophic levels.
- Endosulfan is an organic pollutant used as a pesticide in Southern states for cashew crops, which in new banned world over.
- Chernobyl disaster occurred in Ukraine (USSR) 26th April, 1986 due oe explosion of nuclear power station.
- Nitrate fertilisers cause blue baby syndrome or methemoglobinemia.
- Noise pollution is measured in decibels (Generally sound beyond 80 dB is termed as noise).

Some Import Branches of Biology

Branch	Concerned Field
Agriculture	Study of producing crops from the land
Anatomy	Study of the animal forms with an emphasis on human bodies
Anthology	Study of flowers
Anthropology	Study of apes and man
Apiculture	Honey Industry (Bee keeping)
Biochemistry	Deals with the study of chemical reactions in relation to life activities.
Cardiology	Study of heart
Cryogenics	Study concerning with eh application and uses of very low temperature.
Cryogenics	Study of cells.
Dermatology	Study of skin.
Floriculture	Study of flower yielding plants.
Genetics	Study of heredity and variations.
Gerontology	Study of growing old.
Horticulture	Study of garden cultivation.
Myology	Study of muscles.
Nephrology	Study of kidneys.
Obstetrics	Branch of medicine dealing with pregnancy.
Ornithology	Study of birds.
Phycology	Study of algae.
Pedology	Study of soils
Patholgoy	Study of disease causing organisms
Physiology	Science dealing with the study of functions of various parts of organisms.
Pisciculture	Study of fish.
Sericulture	Silk industry (culture of silk moth and pupa).
Serpentology	Study of snakes.
Taxonomy	Study of classification of organisms.
Virology	Study of virus.

PHYSICS

- In Physics, we study about a large number of physical quantities. Physical quantities are broadly classified into two categories : scalars and vectors.
- Scalar Quantities Physical quantities which have magnitude only. e.g., Mass, speed, volume, work, time, power, energy, etc. are scalar quantities.
- Vector Quantities Physical quantities, which have magnitude and direction both, e.g., Displacement, velocity, acceleration, force, momentum, torque etc.

- For a quantity to be a vector, it is necessary that it follows the triangle rule of addition of two vector.

Newton's Laws of Motion

- First Law Every body maintains its initial state of rest or uniform motion on a straight line unless any external force acts on it. it is also called Galileo's law of inertia.
- Example While jumping from a slowly moving train/bus one must run for a short distance, in the direction fo motion.
- Second Law The force acting on an object is directly proportional to the product of the mass of the object and the acceleration produced on it.
- Third Law To every action, there is an equal and opposite reaction.
- Example Bogies of the trains are provided with buffers to avoid sever jerks during shunting of trains.
- Rocket moves up de to the reaction of downward ejection of gas.

Circular Motion

- When an object moves along a circular path, its motion is called circular motion.
- The direction of motion at any pont in circular motion is given by the tangent to the circle at that point.
- The external force required to act radially inward over the circular motion of the body is called centripetal force.
- In the death well, the walls of well exert an inward force over the motorcycle and as a reaction, the motorcycle exert an outward force on the walls of the well.
- Centrifugal force is such a pseudo force that is equal and opposite to centripetal force.
- Cream separator, centrifugal dryer work on the principle of centrifugal force.

Friction

- It is the opposing force that is set-up between the surface of contact of two bodies when one body slides or rolls our tends to do so on the surface of another body.
- Due to friction we are able to move on the surface of Earth.
- On applying brakes in automobiles,l it stops only due to friction.

Work

- Work is said to be done, if force acting on a body is able to actually move it through some distance in the direction of the force. Its SI unit is **joule**.

Work = FZ cos 0

- where, force, displacement and is the angle between the direction of force and displacement.
- If $\theta>90°$, then work will be negative.
- If $\theta<90°$, then work will be positive.
- If $\theta=90°$, then work will be zero.
- If a coolie carrying a load on his head is moving on a horizontal platform, then theoretically he is not doing any work because ,

Energy

- Capacity of doing work by a body is called its energy. Energy is a scalar quantity and its units is joule. Mechanical energy is of two types.
- Kinetic Energy Energy possessed by a body due to its motion.

$$K = \frac{1}{2}mv^2$$

where, is mass and is the velocity.

- **Potential Energy (U)** The capacity of doing work developed in a body due to its position or configuration.

U = mgh

where, is mass, is acceleration due to gravity and is height.

- The sum of all kinds of energies in an isolated system remains constant at all times. This is the law of conservation of energy.

Power

- Rate of doing work is called power. Its unit is watt.

$$\text{Power} = \frac{\text{Work done}}{\text{Time taken}}$$

- 1 watt hour = 3600 joule

- 1 kilowatt hour = 3.6×60^6 joule
- 1 HP = 746 watt

Gravitation

- Everybody in the universe attracts other body by a force called force fo gravitation.
- The gravitational force of the earth is called gravity.
- Gravity is the of earth by which earth pulls a body towards it centre.
- The acceleration produced in a body due to force fo gravity is called acceleration due to gravity (g) and its value is 9.8 m/s^2.
- Acceleration due to gravity is independent of shape, size and mass of the body.
- Escape velocity is the minimum velocity with which an object just crosses the Earth's gravitational field and never returns. Escape velocity at the Earth's surface is 11.2 km/s.
- Escape velocity at the Moon's surface is 2.4 km/s. Due to law escape velocity there is no atmosphere on the Moon.
- Value of 'g' decreases with height or depth from earth's surface.
  - g is maximum at poles.
  - g is minimum at poles.
  - g decreases due to rotation of Earth.
- g decreases if angular speed of Earth increases and increases if angular speed of Earth decreases.
- the acceleration due to gravity at the Moon is one-sixth that of the Earth. So, the weight of a person on the surface of the Moon will be one-sixth of his actual weight on the Earth.

Satellites

- Satellites are natural or artificial bodies revolving around a planet under its gravitational force of attraction.
- Moon is a natural satellite, while INSAT-B is an artificial satellite of Earth.
- The period of revolution of satellite revolving near the surface of Earth is 1 hour 24 minutes (84 minutes).
- Geo-stationary satellite revolves around the Earth at a height of 36000 km (approx). The orbit of geo-stationary satellite is called parking orbit. Geo-stationary satellite revolves in equatorial plane from West to East. Time period of rotation of geo-stationary satellite is 24 h.s
- The **Earth** rotates on its axis from West to **East**. This rotation makes the Sun and the stars appears to be moving across the sky from East to West.
- Geo-Stationary satellite is used to telecast TV programmes from of the world to another, in weather forecasting, in predictions of floods and droughts.
- Polar satellite revolves around the Earth in polar orbit at a height of 800 km (approx). Time period of these satellites in 84 min.
- Orbital speed of a satellite is independent of its mass.

General Propertie of Matter

Pressure

- Pressure is defined as forces acting normally on a unit area of the surface.

$$\text{Pressure} = \frac{\text{Force}}{\text{Area}}$$

- Its unit is N/m^2. It si a scalar quantity.
- Atmospheric pressure is measured by an instrument called the barometer.
- Sudden fall in barometric reading is the indication of storm.
- Slow fall in barometric reading is the indication of rain.
- Slow rise in the barometric reading in the indication of clear weather.
- The pressure exerted by liquid column at surface given as **p = hdg**, were is the density of liquid and is height of liquid column. In a static liquid at same horizontal level, pressure is same at all points.
- Atmospheric pressure decreases with altitude
- That is way
  - It is difficult to cook on the mountain.
  - The fountain pen of a passenger leaks in aeroplane.
  - Bleeding occurs for the nose.
  - It is difficult to breath on higher altitude due to less amount partial pressure of oxygen in air.
  - Water starts to boil below 100°C.

Pascal's Law of Pressure

- If gravitational attraction is negligible in equilibrium condition, (approx) pressure is same at tall points in a liquid.
- The pressure created anywhere at a point of confined liquid is transmitted equally and undiminished in all directions throughout the liquid.

Floatation

A body floats in a liquid if

- The density of material of the body is less than or equal to the density of liquid.
- When the density of material of the body is equal to density of liquid, the body floats fully submerged in liquid in neutral equilibrium.
- When body floats in neutral equilibrium, the weight of the body is equal to the weight of displaced liquid. The centre of gravity of the body the centre of gravity of the displaced liquid should be in one vertical line for this condition.

Archimedes' Principle

- When a body is immersed partly or wholly in a liquid, there in an apparent loss in the weight of the body, which is equal to the weight of liquid displaced by the body.
- The weight of water displaced by an iron ball is less than its own weight whereas water displaced by the immersed portion of a ship is equal to its weight. So, small ball of iron ball sink in water, but large ship float.
- A fat person will quickly learn the swimming as compared to a slim persons because he will displace more water. So, he will be more balanced.
- Hydrogen filled balloon float in air because hydrogen is lighter than air.
- A person can lift more weight in water.

Density

- Density is defined as mass per unit volume.
- Relative density is measured by hydrometer.
- The density of sea water is more than that of normal water.
- When a ship enters is a sea from a river, it raise a bit because the density of saline water (salt water) is higher.
- The density of iron is more than that of water, but less than that of mercury. So, a solid chunk of iron sink in water but float in mercury.
- If ice floating in water in a vessel melts, the level of water in the vessel dose not change.

Surface Tension

- It is the force acting normally on unit length of imaginary8 line drawn on the surface of liquid i.e.,$T = F/l$, its unit in N/m.
- The property of a liquid by virtue of which it tries to minimise its free surface area is called the surface tension.
- Surface tension decreases with rise in temperature and becomes zero at the critical temperature.
- The surface tension of clean water is higher than that of a soap solution.
- Formation of lead shots, spraying result in coldness, floating of needle on water, dancing of camphor on water, are based on surface tension.
- Rain drop form spherical shape due to surface tension.
- When kerosene oil is sprinkled on water, its surface tension decreases, due to which the excess of mosquitoes floating on the surface of water die due to sinking.

Cohesive and Adhesive Forces

Force of attraction applied between molecules of same substance is called cohesive force while attractive force between molecules of different substance is called adhesive force.

Capillarity

- The phenomenon of rise or depression of liquids in a capillary tube is called capillarity.
- A piece of blotting paper soaks ink because the pores of the blotting paper save as capillary tubes.
- The oil in the wick of a lamp rises due to capillary action of threads in the wick.
- The root hairs of plants drawn water form the soil through capillary action.

Viscosity

- Viscosity is the property of a fluid by virtue of which an internal fractional force between its layers, when it is in motion.

Bernoulli's Theorem

- When an incompressible and non-viscous (or gas) flows in streamlined motion form one place to another, then at every point of its path the total energy per unit volume (pressure energy + kinetic energy + potential energy) is constant.
- Venturimeter, Atomizer, filter pump, motion of aeroplane are based upon the Bernoulli's theorem.

Heat and Thermodynamics

Heat

- Heat is a form of energy, which measures the sensation or perception of warmness or coldness of a body or environment.
- Its units are calorie, kilocalorie or joule.
- 1 calorie = joule.

Temperature

- Temperature is the measurement of hotness or coldness of a body.
- When two bodies are placed in contact, heat always flow from a body at higher temperature to the body at loser temperature.
- An instrument used to measure the temperature of a body is called a thermometer.
- The normal temperature of a human body is 37°C or 98.4F°C.
- -40° is the temperature at which Celsius and Fahrenheit thermometers read same.
- The clinical thermometer reads from 96°F to 110°F.
- White roof keeps the house cooler in summer than black roof because white roof reflects more and absorbs less heat rays whereas black roof absorbs more and reflects less heat rays.
- Ice wrapped in a blanket does not melt away quicky because woollen blanket is a bad conductor of heat.
- Silver is the best conductor of heat.
- Cooking untensils are made of aluminium, brass and steel because these substances have low specific heat and high conductivity.

Thermal Expansion

- Thermal expansion is the increase in size on heating.
- A solid can undergo three types of expansions
  - (i) Linear expansion
  - (ii) Superficial expansion
  - (iii) Cubical expansion
- Telephone wires are kept loose to allow the wire for contraction in winter.
- A gap is provides between two iron tracks of the railway track, so that rails can easily expand during summer and do not bend.

Specific Heat

- The amount of heat required to raise the temperature of unit mass of a substance through 1°C, is called its specific heat.
- When temperature of water is increased from 0°C, then its volume decreases upto 4°C, becomes minimum at 4°C and then increases.
- This behaviour of water around 4°C is called anomalous expansion of water.

Latent Heat

- The heat energy absorbed or released at constant temperature per unit mass for change of state is called latent heat.
- Latent heat of fusion of ice of 80 cal/g.
- Latent heat of vaporisation of steam is 536 cal/g.
- How water burns are less serve than that of steam burns because steam has high latent heat.

Evaporation

- It is the slow process of conversion of liquid into its vapour even below its boiling temperature.
- The amount of water vapour in air is called humidity.
- Relative humidity is measured by hygrometer.
- Relative humidity increases with the increase of temperature.

Transmission of Heat

- Transfer of heat from one place to other place is called Transmission of heat.
- In solids, transmission of heat takes place

by conduction process.

- In liquids and gases, transmission of heat takes place by convection process. In room, ventilators are provided to escape the hot air convention.
- Heat from the Sun reaches the Earth by radiation.

Elasticity

Elasticity is the property of material of a body by virtue of which the body acquires its original shape and size after the removal of deforming force.

- A force, which changes the configuration of a body, is called a deforming force.
- Steel is more elastic then rubber.

Simple Pendulum

- Simple pendulum is a heavy point mass suspended from a rigid support by means of an elastic and inextensible string.
- The maximum time period of a simple pendulum is 84.6 min.
- Time taken in one oscillation is called 'time period'.
- The time period of a simple pendulum does not depend upon the mass, shape and size of the bob and its amplitude of oscillation. A pendulum clock goes slow in summer and fast in winter.
- If a simple pendulum is suspended in a lift descending down with acceleration, then time period of pendulum will increase. If lift is ascending. then time period of pendulum will decrease.
- If a lift falling freely under gravity, then the time period of the pendulum is infinite

WAVES

- A wave is disturbance, which propagates energy form one place to the other without the transportation of matter.
- Waves are broadly of two types
  (i) Mechanical wave (longitudinal wave and transverse wave)
  (ii) Electromagnetic wave

Longitudinal Waves

- In this wave, the particles of the medium vibrate in the direction of propagation of wave.
- Waves on springs or sound waves in air are examples of longitudinal waves.

Transverse Waves

- In this wave, the particles of the medium vibrate perpendicular to the direction of propagation of wave.
- Waves on strings under tension, waves on the surface of water are the examples of transverse waves.

Electromagnetic Waves

- The waves, which do not require medium for their propagation i.e., which can propagate even through the vacuum are called electromagnetic waves.
- Light radio waves, X–rays, etc. are the examples of electromagnetic waves. These wave propagate with the velocity of light in vacuum.

Sound Waves

Sound waves are longitudinal mechanical waves. Based on their frequency range sound waves are divided into following categories.

- The sound waves which lie in the frequency range 20 Hz to 20000 Hz are called audible waves.
- The sound waves having frequencies loss than 20 Hz are called infrasonic ultrasonic waves.
- Ultrasonic waves are used for sending signals, measuring the depth of sea. cleaning machinery parts located in hard to reach places. such as spiral tubes, etc.

Speed of Sound

- Speed of sound in maximum in solid and minimum n gases.
- When sound goes from one medium to another medium, its speed and wavelength changes, but frequency remains unchanged.
- The speed of sound remains unchanged by the increase of decreases of pressure.
- The speed of sound increase with the increase of temperature of the medium.
- The speed of sound is more in humid air than in dry air because the density of humid air is less then the density.
- **Echo** The repetition of sound due to reflection of sound waves. is called echo.
- **Intensity** It is defined as the amount of energy passing per unit time through a unit area that is per perpendicular to

the direction in which sound waves are travelling.

- **Pitch** The sensation of a frequency is commonly referred to as the pitch of a sound.
- **SONAR** It stands for sound navigation and ranging. It is used to measure the depth of a sea, to locate the enemy submarines and shipwrecks.

Doppler's Effect

- If there is a relative motion between source of sound and observer, the apparent frequency of sound heard by the observer is different from the actual frequency of sound emitted by the source. This phenomenon is called Doppler's effect.
- When the distance between the source and observer decreases, then apparent frequency increases vice–versa.

Light

- Light is a form of energy, which is propagated as electromagnetic wave.
- It is the radiation which makes our eyes able to see the object. Its speed is 3 ×10 m/s. It is the form energy. It is a transverse wave. It takes 8 min 19 s to reach on the Earth from the Sun and the light reflected from Moon takes 1.28 s to reach Earth.

Reflection of Light

- When a ray of light falls on a boundary separating who media comes black into the same medium. Then this phenomenon is called reflection of light

Laws of Reflection

- The incident ray, reflected ray and the normal to the reflecting surface at the incident point all lie in the same plane.
- The angle of reflection is equal to the angle of incidence.

Reflection from Plane Mirror

- The image is virtual and laterally inverted.
- The size of image is equal to that of object.
- If an object moves towards a plane mirror with speed , relative to the object the image moves towards it with a speed 2.
- To see his full image in a plane mirror, a person requires a mirror of atleast half of his height.
- Then number of images formed by two plane mirrors, inclined by an angle θ,

$$n = 360/\theta - 1$$

Spherical Mirror

- Spherical mirrors are fo two types
  (i) Concave mirror (ii) Convex mirror
- Image formed by a convex mirror is always virtual, erect and diminished.
- Image formed by a concave mirror is generally real and inverted.

Uses of Concave Mirror

(i) As a shaving glass, (ii) As a reflector for the headlights of a vehicle, search light. (iii) In ophthalmoscope to examine eye, ear, nose by doctors. (iv) In solar cookers.

Uses of Convex Mirror

(i) As a rear view mirror in vehicle because it provides the maximum rear field of view and image formed is always erect. (ii) In sodium reflector lamp.

Refraction of Light

- The bending of the ray of light passing from one medium to other medium is called refraction. When a ray of light enters from one medium to other medium. Its frequency and phase do not change, but wavelength and velocity change. Due to refraction from Earth's atmosphere, the stars appear to twinkle.
- Refractive index (μ)

$$= \frac{\text{Speed of light in vacuum}}{\text{Speed of light in the medium}}$$

Critical Angle

- The angle of incidence in a denser medium for which the angle of refraction in rarer medium becomes 90°, is called the critical angle.

Total Internal Reflection (TIR)

- If light is travelling from denser medium to rarer medium and the angle of incidence is more than the critical angle, then the light is reflected back into the denser medium. This phenomenon is called total internal reflection.

- Sparking of diamond, mirage and looming, shinning of air bubble in water and optical fibre are examples of total internal reflection.

Optical Fibre

- It works on the principal TIR. It is used for telecommunication and various medical purposes like endoscopy.

Lens

- Lens is generally of two types
  (i) Convex lens
  (ii) Concave lens
- When lens a dipped in a liquid of higher refractive index, the focal length increases and convex lens behave as concave lens and vice–versa
- An air bubble trapped in water or glass appears as convex, but behaves as concave lens.

Dispersion of Light

- When a ray of white light is passed through a prism, it gets splitted into its constituent colours. This phenomenon is called dispersion of light.
- The different colours appeared in the spectrum are in the following order, violet, indigo, blue green, yellow, orange and red (VIBGYOR).
- Rainbow is formed due to dispersion of sunlight by water droplets.
- Wavelength of red colour is maximum and for violet colour is minimum.
- Red, green and blue are primary colours. Green and magenta, blue and yellow, red and cyan are complementary colours.

Scattering of Light

- When light passes through a medium in which particles are suspended whose size are of the order of wavelength of light, then light striking on these particles deviated in different directions, Scattering of light is maximum in case of violet colour and minimum in case of red colour.
- Blue colour of sky is due to scattering of blue and violet light. The brilliant red colour of rising and setting sun is also due to scattering of light.

Human Eye

- It is an optical instrument like camera. It forms the real image of the object on retina of the eye. Least distance of distinct vision is 25 cm.

Defects of Eye

Myopia (Short sigtedness)	A short sighted eye can see only nearer objects. Distant objects are not seen clearly. This defect can be removed by using concave lens of suitable focal length
Hypermetropia (Long sightedness)	A long sighted eye can see distant objects clearly but nearer object are not clearly visible. This defect can be removed by using a convex lens.
Presbyopia	In this defect both near and far objects are not clearly visible. It can be removed by using bi–focal lens.
Astigmatism	In this defect eye cannot see horizontal and vertical lines clearly. This defect can be removed by using suitable cylindrical lenses.

Microscope

- Simple microscope is a convex lens of small focal length.
- Compound microscope is a combination of tow convex lenses, called objective lens and eyepieces, separated by a distance.
- Astronomical Telescope is also a combination of two lenses in which objective lens si convex lens of large aperture and large focal length while eye–piece is a convex liens of small aperture and small focal length.

Electricity and Magnetism

Charge

- Charge is the basic property associated with matter due to which it produces and experiences electric and magnetic effects. Similar charges repel each other and opposite charges attract each other. The SI unit of charge is **coulomb**.

Conductor	Conductors are those materials. which allow electricity to pass through themselves Metals like sliver, iron, copper and earth acts like a conductor Silver is the best conductor.
Insulator	Insulator are those materials which do not allow electricity to flow through themselves Wood, paper, mica, giass, ebonite and insulators.

Electric Current

- Electric current is defined as the rate of flow of charge or charge flowing per unit time. Its unit is ampere. It si a scalar quantity.
- A lightning conductor fixed on tall buildings to protect them from the destructive effects of the lightning.
- An electric bulb produces a bang when it is broken because there is a vacuum inside the electric bulb, when the bulb is broken air rushes at great speed from all sides to fill the vacuum. The rushing of air produces a noise generally referred to as the bang.

Ohm's Law

- At the constant physical conditions of any conductor, the current flowing through the conductor is directly proportional to the potential difference across it.

  $I = V / R$, where is the resistance.

- If a wire is stretched, its resistance will change but its specific resistance will remina unaffected.
- On increasing the temperature of the metal, its resistance increases.
- On increasing the temperature of semiconductor, its resistance decreases.
- On increasing the temperature of electrolytes, its resistance decreases.
- The reciprocal of resistivity of a conductor is called its conductivity its unit is mho m^{-1}.
- The heating effect of electric current is known as Joule's law of heating.
- Electric bulb, electric kettle, heater, etc devices work on the bases of heating effect of electric current.
- Ammeter It is a device which is used to measure electrical current. It is connected in series. The resistance of an ideal ammeter is zero.
- Voltmeter It is a device used to measure the potential difference between two points in a circuit. It is connected in parallel to the circuit.
- The resistance of an ideal voltmeter is infinite.
- Fuse Wire It is a small conducting wire of alloy of copper, tin and lead having low melting point. So, it is protective device used in series.

Magnets

- Magnet is a piece of iron or other materials that can attract iron containing object and pints toward North when suspended.
- When a magnet is freely suspended, Its one pole always direct towards the North This pole is called North pole. The other pole is called South pole.
- Like poles of a magnet repel each other and unlike poles attract each other.
- A current carrying coil containing a soft iron core, is called an electromagnet, which is utilised in electric bell, telegraph receiver, telephone diaphragm, transformer, dynamo etc.

Atomic and Nuclear Physics

Cathode Rays

- Cathode ray was discovered by Sir William Crooke and its properties are
- These rays travel in straight lines.
- These rays produce fluorescence.
- These rays can penetrate through thin foils of metal and deflected by both electric and magnetic fields.
- These rays have velocity ranging 1/30th to 1/10th of the velocity of light.

Positive or Canal Rays

- These rays were discovered by Goldstein.
- The positive rays consists of positively charged particles.
- These rays travel in straight line.
- These rays are deflected by electric and magnetic fields.
- These rays are capable of producing physical and chemical changes.
- These rays can produce ionisation in gases.

Radioactivity

- Radioactivity was discovered by Henry Becquerel, Madame Curie and Pierre Curie for which they jointly won Noble Prize.
- The nucleus having protons 83 or more are unstable. They emit α, β and γ particles and becomes stable The elements of such nucleus are called radioactive elements and the phenomenon of emission of α, β and γ particles is called radioactivity.
- Robert Pierre and his wife Madame Curie discovered a new radioactive element radium.
- The end product of all natural radioactive elements after emission of radioactive rays is lead.
- With the emission of an β-particle, atomic number is decreased by 2 and mass number is decreased by 4.
- With the emission of a -particle. atomic number is increased by 1 and mass number does not change.

Nuclear Fission

- The nuclear reaction, in which a heavy nucleus splits into the nuclei of nearly equal mass in nuclear fission.

$$ {}_{93}U^{235} + {}_{0}n^{1} \rightarrow {}_{56}Ba^{141} $$
$$ + {}_{36}Kr^{92} + {}_{30}n^{1} + \text{energy} $$

- Atom Bomb is based on nuclear fission. U^{235} and are used as fissionable material.
- Nuclear fission was first demonstrated by Hatin and Fritz Strassmann.

Nuclear Fusion

- When two ro more light nuclei combined together to form a heavier nucleus is called as nuclear fusion.
- For the nuclear fusion, a temperature of the order of 10^8 K is required.
- Hydrogen Bomb was made by the American Scientist in 1952. This is based on nuclear fusion. It is 1000 times more powerful than atom bomb.

Nuclear Reactor or Atomic Pile

- Nuclear reactor is an arrangement, in which controlled nuclear fission reaction takes place.
- First nuclear reactor was established in Chicago University under the supervision of Prof Enrico Fermi.
- Heavy water, graphite and beryllium oxide are used to slow down the fast moving neutrons. They are called moderator.
- The cold water, liquid oxygen, etc. are used as coolant to remove heat generated.
- Cadmium or boron rods are good absorber of neutrons and called the control rods.

Uses of Nuclear Reactor

(i) To produce electrical energy from the energy released during fission.

(ii) To produce different isotopes, which can be used in medical, physical and agriculture science.

- There are several components of nuclear reactor which are as follows.
- Fissionable Fuel U^{235} or U^{239} isl used.
- Moderator Moderator decreases the energy of neutrons, so that they can be further used for fission reaction. Heavy water and graphite are used as moderator.
- Control Rod Rods of cadmium or boron are used to absorb the excess neutrons produced in fission of uranium nucleus, so that the chain reaction continues to be controlled.
- Coolant A large amount of heat is produced during fission. Coolant absorbs that heat and prevents excessive rise in the temperature. The coolant may be water, heavy water or a gas like He or CO_2.

LASSER (Light Amplification by Stimulated Emission of Radiation)

- It is a device that produces an intense, coherent and highly directional beam of the single frequency. It can be transmitted over a great distance without being spread.

LASER Technology in India

- In 1964, the first laser as gallium Arsenide (GaA) semi-conductor laser was designed and fabricated by Bhabha Atomic Research Centre (BARC)
- Various Institutions as CAT (Centre for Advanced Technology), DRDO (Defence Research and Development Organisation) and Indian Institute of Science work on the laser plasma, quantum optics, etc., are going to work American collaboration..
- MASER (Microwave Application by Stimulated Emission of Radiation) It was invented three American scientist Gordon, Gieyer and H Townes in 1952. It used microwaves in amplified form of longer wavelength of the light, while ordinary laser used light.

CHEMISTRY

- Chemistry, a branch of physical science, is which deals with the composition, properties and behaviours of matter.
- A French Chemist Cavoisier (1743-1793) is regarded as father of maodern Chemistry.

Physical and Chemical Changes

- Physical changes are the changes which only affect the physical properties like colour, density, melting point etc, of matter, but do not affect the composition and chemical properties of matter.
- A physical change is temporary, while a chemical change is permanent.
- Crystallisation, sublimation, boiling, melting, vaporisation, cutting of trees, dissolving sugar or salt in water etc are physical changes.
- Chemical changes affect the composition as well as chemical properties of matter and result in the formation of a new substance.
- Burning of fuel, burning of candle and paper, electrolysis of water, photosynthesis, ripening of fruits etc, are examples of chemical changes.

Matter

- Matters have three states Solid, Liquid and Gaseous.
- Researchers discussing for another two states of matters Plasma (Ionised gases containing super energetic and super excited particles) and Bose-Einstein Condensates or BEC (a gas at super low temperature with extremely low density).

Boiling Point

- The temperature at which liquid converts into vapour is called its boiling point.
- Boiling point of water is 100°C.
- The boiling point increases in the presence of impurities that's why boiling point of sea water is more than the boiling point of pure water (as the former contains impurity).
- It usually decreases at high altitudes. That's why at high altitude, the boiling point of water is less than 100°C and more time is required to cook a food.

Melting Point

- It is a temperature at which a substance converts from its solid state to liquid state. Melting point of ice is 0°C. It decrease in the presence of impurity.

Atom, Molecule and Element

- An atom is the smallest particle of the element that can exist independently and retain all its chemical properties.
- Atom is made up of electrons, protons and neutrons.
- Protons and neutrons reside in the nucleus (at the centre of atom)s whereas electrons revolve around the nucleus.
- A molecule is the smallest part of an element or a compound cabable or independent existence under ordinary conditions.
- Elements contains only one type of atoms, e.g. carbon (C), sulphur (S), diamond, graphite etc.
- Ununseptium (a superheavy chemical element with atomic number 117) is a member of group-17 in the periodic table below the five halogens (fluorine, chlorine, bromine, iodine and astatine). Its synthesis was claimed in Dubna, Russia by a joint Russian-American collaboration.
- In 2014, the GSI Helmboltz Centre for Heavy Ion Research in Germany also claimed to have successfully repeated original experiment.

Isotopes and Isobars

- Isotopes have the same number of protons (atomic number), but different number of neutrons and mass number (atomic number number of neutrons), e.g. $_1H^1$, $_1H^2$, $_1H^3$.
- Isobars have the same mass number but different atomic number. e.g. $_{18}H^{40}$. $_{19}H^{40}$, and $_{20}H^{40}$.

Dating Techniques

- Radiocarbon dating is used to determine the age of carbon bearing materials like wood, animal fossils etc.
- Uranium dating is used to determine the age of Earth, minerals and rocks.

Colloids

- These are heterogeneous solutions, containing two phases : dispersed phase and dispersion medium.
- These show Tyndall effect (i.e. scattering of light by colloidal particles) and Brownian motion (zig-zag motion).
- Colloids can be dispersion medium loving (i.e. lyophilic) or dispersion medium repelling (i.e. lyophobic)

Some Colloids and their Example

Dsspersed Phase	Dispersion Medium	Type of Colloid	Example
Liqid	Gas	Aerosol	Fog, clouds, mist
Solid	Gas	Aerosol (solid)	Smoke, automobile exhaust
Gas	Liquid	Foam	Shaving cream
Liquid	Liquid	Emulsion	Milk, face cream
Liquid	Solid	Sol	Mud, milk of magnesia
Gas	Solid	Foam	Foam, rubber, sponge, pumice
Liquid	Solid	Gel	Jelly, cheese, butter
Solid	Solid	Solid sol	Milky glass, coloured gem stone

Battery

Battery is a device, used to convert chemical energy and is of two types :

- Primary batteries (non-rechargeable) act as galvanic cell, e.g. dry cell, mercury cell etc.
- Secondary batteries (rechargeable) act as galvanic as well as voltaic cell e.g. lead storage battery, nickel cadmium battery etc.
- In electrolytic refining, anode is made by impure metal and a strip of pure metal acts as cathode.s

Types of Batteries

Battery	Anode	Cathode	Electrolyte	Used in
Leclanche cell	Zinc	Graphite	Paste of ammonium chloride and zinc chloride	Transistors, clocks
Mercury cell	Zinc-mercury amalgam	Paste of HgO (Mercuric oxide) and carbon	Paste of KOH and ZnO	Hearing aids
Lead storage battery	Lead	Lead packed in lead dioxide	38% solution of sulphuric acid	Automobiles, invertors

Corrosion

- A sliced apple, when exposed to air, turns brown after sometime. This is because apple contains iron, which gets oxidised and gives a brownish colour to apple.

Renewable and Non-renewable Natural Resources

- A renewable resource is a resource which can be used repeatedly because it is replaced naturally. Renewable resources are available in large excess, i.e. never ends, e.g. air, sunlight etc.
- Non-renewable resources are available in limited quantity and end, if used excessively, after a limited period of time, e.g. mineral, coal, petroleum, natural gas etc.

Coal

- Coal is obtained by carbonisation of vegetable matter and is available in different varieties : Peat (60% C), lignite or brown coal (70% C), bituminous coal (60% to 80% C), anthracite coal (90% C). Out of these, bituminous is the most common form.

Calorific Value of Some Substances

Fuel	Calorific Value (kJ/g)
Coal	25-32
Kerosene oil	48
Petrol	50
Diesel	45
Biogas	35-40
LPG	50
Cow dung	6-8
Hydrogen	50
Natural gas	33-50

Safety Matches

- In safety matches, the stick consists of a mixture of antimony trisulphide and potassium chlorate at its one end. the box side contains a mixture of powdered glass and red phosphorus.

Acids, Bases and Salts

Acids

- These are the substance, which have a sour taste and turn blue litmus red.
- These are good conductor of electricity in aqueous solution.
- Pickels are always kept in glass jar because acid present in them reacts with metal to produce hydrogen gas.

Bases

- These are the substances, which have bitter taste, soapy to touch and turn red litmus blue.
- Bases the NaOH, KOH, etc. are good conductors of electricity in their aqueous solution and in molten state.
- Base reacts with acid to form salt and water.

Salts

- These are the product of neutralisation reaction between an acid and a base.
- pH is the measure of acidity/basicity.

Some Important Compounds in Everyday Life

Carbon Dioxide (CO)

- In is an acidic oxide of carbon and is used by green plants for photosynthesis. It does not help in burning.
- Air and our breath contains carbon dioxide. Thus, when lime water is kept in air or we pass our breath into it, the lime water turns milky.

Carbon Monoxide (Co)

- It is a neutral oxide of air and has more affinity towards haemoglobin than oxygen (about 200 times more). That's why in the environment of carbon monoxide (which is a non-poisonous gas) people die for the need of oxygen.
- It is dangerous to sleep in abn unventilated room with fire burning inside because the fire produce carbon monoxide and carbon dioxide gases.

Plaster of Paris (CaSO.HO)

$$\left(CsSO_4.\frac{1}{2}H_2O\right)$$

- It is chemically calcium sulphate hemihydrate (CaSO. HO) and is prepared by heating gypsum which is calcium sulphate dehydrate ($CaSO_4.1/2\ H_2O$) at 373 K.

- On mixing with water, Plaster of Paris further sets into a hard solid, called gypsum. Thus, it is used to plaster fractured bones, for making toys, materials for decoration and for making surfaces smooth.

Portland Cement

- It is a complex mixture of silicates and aluminate of calcium with small amount of gypsum. Raw material used for the manufacture of Portland cement are limestone and clay.
- The composition of Portland cement is calcium oxide (50-60%), alumina (5-10%), and magnesium oxide (2-3%) Gypsum is added to cement to decrease its rate of setting.
- In cement, if lime is in excess, cement cracks during setting and if lime is less, cement is of weak strength.
- Mortar a mixture of sand, cement and water is used for joining brikcs and plastering walls.
- Concrete, a mixture of gravel, sand, cement and water is used for flooring and making roads.
- Reinforced Concrete Cement (RCC) which is concrete with steel bars and wires is used for constructing roofs, bridges and pillars.

Soaps

- These are sodium and potassium salts of higher fatty acids, e.g. sodium palmitate, sodium stearate, etc.

Glass

- Glass, an amorphous solid or super-cooled liquid contains maninly silica (SiO).

Colour	Substance Added
Red	Copper oxide (CuO)
Green	Chromium oxide (CrO)
Ruby Red	Goldchloride (AuCl)
Blue	Cobalt oxide (CoO)
Brown	Iron oxide (FeO)

Pesticides

- These chemicals are used to destroy the organisms that harm the crop.
- These are of following types
- Insecticides e.g. DDT, gammaxene, aluminium phosphate.
- Fungicides e.g. Bordeaux mixture, organo-mercury compounds.
- Herbicides e.g. Benzipram, sodium chlorate.
- Rodenticides e.g. Aluminium phosphide.
- Heavy Water
- Heavy water is deuterium oxide (D_2O), (molecular mass = 20) which used as moderator in nuclear reactors. It is called heavy due to the presence of deuterium, the heavy hydrogen.

Hard Water

- The water in which soluble bicarbonates of calcium and magnesium are present, is called temporary hard water and in which soluble sulphates and chlorides or magnesium and calcium are present is called permanent hard water.
- The temporary hardness of water is removed by boiling or by adding calcium hydroxide, $Ca(OH)_2$—the Clark's process.
- the permanent hardness of water is removed by adding sodium carbonate CO), or calgon (sodium hexametaphosphate, $Na_2[Na_4(PO_3)_6]$.

Hardening of Oil (Hydrogenation)

- Oil, an unsaturated fat when heated with nickel catalyst and hydrogen, gets converted into a solid mass called ghee, a saturated fat. This process is called hardening of oil and is carried out through hydrogenation in the presence of nickel as a catalyst.

Polymers

- A polymer is a compound of high molecular weight formed by the combination of a larger number of molecules on one or two types of low molecular weight (known as monomers) and the process is called polymerisation.

Medicines

These are the chemicals used for treating diseases and reducing suffering from pain.

Different Medicines and their Examples

Medicine	Medicine	Example
Analgesic	Reduce pain	Aspirin, paracetamol, morphine, phenacetin
Tranquilizer	To treat stress, mild and severe mental diseases	Equanil, Valium, chlorodiazeopoxide, serotonin and meprobamate
Antiseptic	Prevent the growth of micro-organisms or kill them (applied to living tissues)	Dettol (a mixture of chloroxylenol—the antiseptic and -terpineol), savlon, iodine tincture (solution of I alcohol water mixture), boric acid (antiseptic for eyes), hydrogen peroxide, iodoform
Antibiotic	Destroy microorganisms (These are obtained from microorganisms)	Penicillin (discovered by A Fleming in 1929, amipicillin, amoxicillin, ofloxiacin, chloramphenicol)
Antimalarial	Cure malaria	Chloroquine
Sulphadrugs	Alternative for antibiotics	Sulphanilamide, sulphadiazine
Antacids	Reduce acidity	Baking soda, magnesium hydroxide

COMPUTER

A computer is An electronic machine which stores, reads and processes data to produce meaningful information as output is called Computer.

Components of Computer

- Input Unit Devices used to give instructions, Keyboard, Mouse, Joystick, Optical character reader, CDs, Bar code reader, Touch screen, Light pen, Scanner, Magnetic Ink Character Recognition (MICR), etc.
- Central Processing Unit (CPU) is the device for the manipulation of information inside the computer. CPU is known as the brain of the computer, but commonly called a processor and has the following components.
- Arithmetic Logic Unit (ALU) performs all logical and arithmetical operations.
- Control Unit (CU) instructs, maintains and controls the flow of information.
- Output Unit is the device to display the result of processing, e.g. Visual Display Unit, Printer, Monitor, Speaker, Pen Driver, etc.

Memory

- Memory holds all the raw and processed data, set of instructions and information inside the CPU.

Primary Memory

- Primary Memory stores the data which is currently in used by the computer.
- **RAM** (Random Access Memory) It is a volatile memory. It is a temporary storage.
- **DRAM** Dynamic Random Access Memory
- **SRAM** Static Random Access Memory
- **ROM** (Read Only Memory) It is a non-volatile memory where all logical data is stored that cannot bo changed.
- **PROM** Programmable Read Only Memory.
- **EPROM** Erasable Programmable Read Only Memory.
- **EEPROM** Electrically Erasable Programmable Read Only Memory.

Secondary Memory

- It stores data, program, instruction and information permanently.

Hardware

- Any peripheral device which can be seen and touched in hardware. Computer hardware includes input devices, output devices, storage devices and processing devices.

Software

- It is a set fo instructions that directs the computer to process information. It can be classified as
- System Software It is background software that helps that computer to manage its own internal resources. e.g. Operating system, Device driver and Language Translator, etc.
- Application Software is a set of programs designed for specific uses or applications, e.g. word processor, spreadsheets, accounting programs etc.

Networking

- Computer networking relates to the communication between a group of two ro more computers linked together. Most common examples of networking is Internet, connecting millions of people all over the world together. According to scale or size, computer network can be categorised in three ways.
- Local Area Network (LAN) Graphical area spread over 1 km to 10 km or within a same building.
- Metropolitan Area Network (MAN) Graphical area spread over a city or town.
- Wide Area Network (WAN) Graphical area over countries.

Security Threats

- **Worm** It is a self contained program and does not need to be a part of another program to propagate itself.
- **Spam** Spam is an unsolicited message sent over the Internet in the form of e-mails, to a large number of users for the purpose of spreading malware, advertising phishing, etc.
- **Spyware** It is a type of malicious software installed on computers and collects information about users without their knowledge an may send such information to another entity.
- **Malware** A software which is specifically designed to disrupt or damage a computer system. It is a superset of computer viruses, worms, spyware, trojan horses and other malicious orj unwanted software.
- **Virus** A virus is difined as a program or a piece of code that gets loaded onto the computer without users knowledge and replicates itself, e.g. Creeper, Stuxnet, Melissa, Conficker, Code red, SQL Slammer, Nimada (derived from the word 'Admin'), etc.

Antivirus

Antivirus is a software consisting of computer programs that attempt to identify, defect and prevent the malware from the computer.

Super Computers Developed in India

Super Computer	Year	Mft Company
Param Kanchenjunga	2016	CDAC & NIT Sikkim
Param Ishan	2016	DAC & IIT Guwahati
Aaditya	2013	Indian Institute of Tropical Meteorology
PARMA YUVA II	2011	C-DAC, PUNE
SAGA-220	2011	ISRO
ANUPAM-Adhya	2010-2011	BARC
PARAM YUVA	2008	C-DAC, PUNE

Super Computers of the World

Name	Year	Country	Operating System
Sunway Taihulight	2016	China	Linux
Tianhe-2	2013	China	Kyline Linux
Titan	2012	America	Linux
Sequoia	2011	America	Linux
K-Computer	2011	Japan	Linux
Mira	2010	America	Linux

GENERAL KNOWLEDGE

FIRST IN THE WORLD

First Radio Telescope Satellite launched into Space	HALCA (Japan)
First country to use Glass	Egypt and Mesopotamia
First country to make Map	Mesopotamia (Greece)
First Spaceship landed on Marsh	Viking-I (July 1976)
World's First Multipurpose River Valley Project	Tennessee River Valley Project (USA)
First Space Shuttle Launched	Columbia (April 1981)
First Rocket to go near the Sun	Helius 'B'
First Country to make Constitution	America
First Country to start Underground Metro Rail	Britain
First Unmanned Mission on the Moon	LUNA-9
First Spacecraft to carry man on the Moon	Apollo-11
First Country to do Artificial Satellite Experiment	Russia
Country to give Voting Right to Women	New Zealand
First Country to appoint Lokpal Sweden	Sweden
First Country to imposed Carbon Tax	New Zealand

FIRST IN THE WORLD (MALE)

First Asian to Head the International Cricket Council	Jagmohan Dalmiya
First man to climb Mount Everest	Sherpa Tenzing Norgay and Sir Edmund Hillaryu (29th Mya, 1953)
First Man to go into Space	Major Yuri Gagarin (USSR) (1961)
First Main to walk into Space	Alexei Leonov (Russia)
First Person to give information about Planets and their motion around the Sun	Nicolous Copernicus
First Man to compile Encyclopedia	Aspheosis (Athens)

First person to go on both the Poles (North and South)	Ranulph Fiennes
First Man to reach North Pole	Robert Peary
First Man to reach South Pole	Roald Amundsen
First Man to climb on Mt Everest without Oxytgen	Phu Dorji Sherpa

FIRST IN THE WORLD (FEMALE)

First Woman President of a Country	Maria Estela Peron (Argentina)
First Woman in the world to cross the Strait of Gibralter	Arti Pradhan (India)
First Woman Cosmonaut in Space	Valenktina Tereshkiova (USSR)
First Woman Prime Minister	Sirimavo Bandaranaike (Sri Lanka)
First Woman to cross the Seven Seas	Bula Choudhary
First Non-white female to win Nobel Prize in Literature	Toni Morrison
First Woman to reach Antarctica	Caroline Mikkelsen
First Woman to have a Space-Walk	Svetlana Yevgengevna Savitskaya

Countries with Capitals and Currencies

Country	Capital	Currency
Afghanistan	Kabul	Afghani
Albania	Tirana	Lek
Algeria	Algires	Algerian Dinar
Angola	Luanda	Kwanza
Argentina	Buenos Aires	Peso
Australia	Canberra	Australian Dollar
Austria	Vienna	Euro
Bangladesh	Dhaka	Taka
Belarus	Minsk	Ruble
Belgium	Brussels	Euro
Bhutan		Thimphu
Brazil	Brasilia	Cruzeiro Real
Cambodia	Phnom-Penh	Riel
Canada	Ottawa	Canadian Dollar
Chile	Santiago	Peso
China	Beijing	Yuan, Renminbi
Colombia	Bogota	Colombian Peso
Danmark	Copenhagen	Krone
Egypt	Cairo	Egyptian Pound
France	Paris	France, Euro
Germany	Berlin	Euro
Greece	Athens	Euro
Hungary	Budapest	Forint
India	New Delhi	Rupees
Indonesia	Jakarta	Rupiah
Iran	Tehran	Rial
Iraq	Baghdad	Dinar

Ireland	Dublin	Euro
Israel	Jerusalem	Shekel
Italy	Rome	Euro
Japan	Tokyo	Yen
Kazakhstan	Astana	Tenge
Kenya	Nairobi	Shilling
North Korea	Pyongyang	Won
Kuwait	Kuwait City	Kuwait Dinar
South Korea	Seoul	Won
Libya	Tripoli	Libyan Dinar
Malaysia	Kuala Lumpur	Ringgit
Maldives	Male	Rufiyaa
Mauritius	Part Louis	Rupee
Mongolia	Ulan Bator	Tugrik
Myanmar	Naypidaw	Kyat
Nigeria	Abuja	Naira
Norway	Oslo	Rupee
Pakistan	Islamabad	Krone
Poland	Budapest	Zloty
Portugal	Lisbon	Euro
Qatar	Doha	Riyal
Russia	Moscow	Ruble
Singapore	Singapore	Dollar
Sri Lanka	Colombo	Sri Lankan Rupee
Taiwan	Taipei	New Talwan Dollar
Thailand	Bangkok	Baht
Turkey	Ankara	Lira
Ukraine	Kiev	Hryvnia
UK	London	Pound Sterling
US	Washington DC	US Dollar
Venezuela	Caracas	Bolivar
Zimbabwe	Harare	US Dollar

Geographical Epithets

Blue Mountains	Nilgiri Hills
City Beautiful	Chandigarh
City of Golden Gate	San Francisco
City of Magnificent Buildings	Washington
City of Palaces	Kolkata
City of Seven Hills	Rome
Cockpit of Europe	Belgium
Dark Continent	Africa
Eternal City	Rome
Forbidden City	Lhasa (Tibet)
Garden City	Chicago
Gift of the Nile	Egypt
Granite City	Aberdeen
Holy Land	Palestine
Island Continent	Australia
Island of Cloves,	Zanzibar
Isle of Pearls	Bahrain
Key to the Mediterranean	Gibraltar
Land of Cakes	Scotland
Land of Golden Fleece	Australia
Land of Maple	Canada
Land of Morning Calm	Korea
Land of the Midnight Sun	Norway
Land of the Rising Sun	Japan

Land of the Thunderbolt	Bhutan
Land of Thousand Lakes	Finland
Land of White Elephant	Thailand
Pearl of the Antilles	Cuba
Parl of the Pacific	Guayaquil Port of Ecuador
Roof of the World	The Pamirs, Central Asia
Spice Garden of India	Kerala
Sugar Bowl of the World	Cuba

Official Books of Major Countries

Blue Book	An official report of the British Government
Green Book	An official publications of Italy and Iran
Grey Book	An official reports of the Governments of Japan and Belgium
Orange Book	An official publications of the Government of Netherlands
White Book	An official publications of China, Germany and Portugal
White Paper	An official paper of the Governments of Britain and India on a particular issue
Yellow Book	An official paper of the Government of France

Important Monuments of Some Famous Countries

Monument	Country	Monument	Monument
Imperial Palace (Tokyo)	Japan	Leaning Tower of Pisa	Italy
Eiffel Tower (Paris)	France	Pyramid (Giza)	Egypt
Great Wall of China	China	Opera House (Sydney)	Australia
Kremlin Palace (Moscow)	Russia	Statue of Liberty (New York)	USA
Kinder Disk	Denmark	Taj Mahal (Agra)	India

The Seven Wonders of the World

Ancient World	Modern World	The 'New' Wonder
The Colossus of Rhodes	Channel Tunnel	Pyramid at Chichen Itza, Mexico
The Great Pyramid of Giza	CN Tower	Christ Redeemer, Brazil
The Hanging Gardens of Babylon	Empire State Building	The Great Wall, China
The Mausoleum of Halicarnassus	Golden Gate Bridge	Machu Picchu, Peru
The Statue of Zeus of Olympia	Itaipu Dam	Petra, Jordan

The Lighthouse of Alexandria	North Sea Protection works	Roman Colosseum, Italy
The Temple of Artemis at Ephesus	Panama Canal	The Taj Mahal, India

Important Symbols or Sings

Pen	Symbol of culture and civilisation
Lotus	Culture and civilisation
Red Cross	Medical aid and hospital
Red Flag	Revolution, also sign of danger
Black Flag	Symbol of protest
Yellow Flag	Flown on ships or vehicles carrying patients suffering from infectious diseases
Flag flown upside down	Symbol of distress
White Flag	Symbol of truce
Pigeon or Dove	Symbol of peace
A blindfolded woman holding a balanced scale	Symbol of justice
Black strip on face arm	Sign of mourning or protest
One skull on two bones crossing each other diagonally	Sign of danger
Wheel (Chakra)	Symbol of of progress
Flag flown at half mast	Symbol of national mourning
Olive Branch	Symbol of peace

Major Newspapers of the World

Newspaper	Country	Newspaper	Country
The Sydney Morning Herald	Australia	The Hindustan Times	India
The Age	Australia	Mainichi Daily News	Japan
Global and Mail	Canada	The New Zealand Herald	New Zealand
The Gazette	Canada	The Press	New Zealand
International Herald Tribune	France	The Times	United Kingdom
Die Welt	Germany	The Scotsman	United Kingdom
The Times of India	India	The Guardian	United Kingdom
The Hindu	India	The Herald	United Kingdom

The Tribune	India	The Courier	United Kingdom
The Statesman	India	Washington Post	United States of America

Parliaments of the World

Country Name	Parliament Name	Country Name	Parliament Name
Afghanistan	Shora	India	Sansad
Australia	Federal Parliament	Japan	Diet
Bangladesh	Jatiyo Shangsad/ House of the Nation	Nepal	Rashtriya Panchayat
Bhutan	Tshogdu	Pakistan	National Assembly and Senate
Canada	Parliament	Russia	Duma
China	National People's Congress	Spain	Cortes
Egypt	Peoples's Assembly	Sweden	Riksdag
France	National Assembly	South Africa	Parliament
Germany	Bundestag	Switzerland	Federal Assembly
Great Britain	Parliament	USA	Congress

FIRST IN INDIA

Newspaper	Bangal Gazette (James Hiceky)
Vernacular Daily	Samachar Darpan
Hindi Newspaper	Udant Martand
Telegraph Line	Diamond Harbour to Kolkata
International Telephone Service	Mumbai to London (1851)
Silent Movie	Raja Harish Chandra (Dadasahbe Phalke 1913)
Talkie Movie	Alam Ara (Andeshir Irani-1931)
Aircraft Carriage Warship	INS Vikrant
Satellite	Aryabhatta (19th April, 1975)
Satellite dedicated exclusively for Education purposes	EDUSAT
Dedicated multi wavelength spacial observatory	Astrosat
Successful indigenous launch vehicle	SLV-3
Nuclear Reactor	Apsara (1956)
Lunar Mission	Chandrayaan-I (October, 2008)
Mars Mission	Mars Orbiter Mission (5th November, 2013)
Hydroelectric Project	Sidrapong (1897)
Asian Games	Delhi (1951)
Census	1872
Regular Decadal Census	1881 Onwards
Biosphere Reserve	Nilgiri
National Park	Hailey National Park (Jim Corbett), 1936
Chairman of UPSE	Ross Barker
E-court	Ahmedabad

Court exclusively dedicated to women	Malda (WB)
Technology Park Thiruvananthapuram	Technopark,
Cloned Animal	Samrupa

First in India (Male)	
First Governor-General of India	William Bentinck (1828)
First and last India govern-General of Free India	C Rajagopalachari
First Commander-in-Chief of Free India	General KM Kariappa
First Field Marshal of India	General SHFJ Manekshaw (1971)
First Indian to go in Space	Rakesh Sharma
First Indian to climb the Mount Everest without Oxygen	Sherpa Ang Dorje
First Indian to become the Managing Direct of World Bank	Gautam Kaji
First Chairman of National Human Rights Commission	Rangnath Mishra
First Indian to get Nobel Prize in Physics	CV Raman (1930)
First Indian to get Nobel Prize in Literature	Rabindranath Tagore (1913)
First Indian to get Nobel Prize in Economics	Dr Amrathy Sen (1998)
First Indian to get Nobel Prize in Medicines (Physiology)	Dr Har Govind Khorana (1968)
First Indian to get Bharat Ratna	Dr S radhakrishnan, C Rajgopalachari and Dr CV Raman (1954)
First Person to be Honoured with the Jnanpitha Award	G Sankare Kurup (Malayalam)
First Person to get Bharat Rantna (Posthumously)	Lal Bahadur Shastri
First Cricketer to get Padma Bhushan	CK Naidu
First Indian to get through ICS	Satyendra Nath Tagore (1869)
First Indian to swim across the English Channel	Mihir Sen (1958)
First Judge of International Court of Justice	Dr. Nagendra Singh

First in India (Female)

First Indian Female Chairperson of Indian National Congress	Sarojini Naidu (1925)
First Woman To climb the Everest	Bachedri Pal (1984)
First Woman Cabinet Minister	Rajkumari Amrit Kaur (1947)
First Woman Chairman of the UN General Assembly	Vijya Laxmi Pandit
First Woman President of India	Pratibha Davi Singh Patill
First Woman Speaker of Lok Sabha	MKeira Kumar (2009)
First Woman Deputy Chairman of Rajya Sabha	Margaret Alva (1962)
First Woman Prime Minster of India	Indira Gandhi
First Woman to reach Antarctica	Meher Moos (1976)
First Woman IAS Officer	Anna Rajam George (1950)
First Woman Chief Justice	Leela Seth (1991)
First Woman to win the Jnanpith Award	Asha Poorna Devi (1976)
First Woman to get the Bharat Ratna	Indira Gandhi
First Female Noble Prize Winner	Mother Teresa (1979)
First Woman to complete Century in World Cup Cricket	Thirush Kamini
First Actress to be nominated to the Rajya Sabha	Nargis Dutt
First Woman Chairman of UPSC	Rose Millian Bethwe (Kharbull)
First Woman nominated to Rajya Sabha	Rukmini Devi Arundale

AWARDS AND HONOURS

International

Noble Prize

- The most prestigious award in the world. It was set-up in 1900 under the will of Alfred Bernhard Nobel.

- The Noble Prizes are presented annually on 10ths December (The death anniversary of the founder).
- It is given in the fields of Peace, Literature, Physics, Chemistry, Physiology or Medicine (from 1901) and Economics (from 1969)

Winners of Noble Prize from India

Winner	Field	Year
Kailash Satyarthi	Peace	2014
Venkatraman Ramakrishnan	Chemistry	2009
Amaratya Sen	Economics	1998
Subrahmanyan Chandrasekhar	Physics	1983
Mother Teresa	Mother Teresa	1979
Hargobin Khorana	Medicine	1968
CV Raman	Physics	1930
Rabindranath Tagore	Literature	1913

Grammy Awards

- It is awarded , for the outstanding achievements in the music industry by National Academy for Recording Arts and Sciences, America,. It weas started in 1959. Pt. Ravi Shanker got this 3 times.

Pulitzer Prize

- Instituted in 1917 and . amed after US publisher Joseph Pulitzer.
- It is conferred annually in the United States for the accomplishments in journalism, literature and music.

Magsdaysay Awards

- Instituted in 1957, Named after Ramon Magsaysay, the former President of Philippines.
- The award is given annually on 31st August, the birth anniversary of Masaysay, for outstanding contributions in Public service, Community Leadership, Journalism, Literature and Creative Arts and International Understanding.

Man Booker Prize

- Instituted in 1968, is the highest literary award of the world, set-up by the Booker Company and the British Pulishers Association along the lines of the Pulitzer Prize of USA.

Right Livelihood Award

- The Right Livelihood Award was established in 1980.
- It is also referred as 'Alternative Noble Prize'.
- It is given to persons to honour those "working on practical and exemplary solutions to the most urgent challenges facing the world today."

Oscar Awards

- Instituted in 1929, these awards are conferred annually by the Academy of Motion Pictures, Arts and Sciences, USA, in recongnition of outstanding contribution in the various field of film making.
- The Indian films nominated for Oscars are Mother India (1957), Salaam Bombay (1988), Lagaan (2001).
- Bhanu Athaiya was the first Indian to win an Oscar Award in 1982 for costume design in Gandhi Movie.

Un Human Rights Award

- Instituted in 1966, this award is given every 5 years for individual contributions to the establishment of human rights.

National

Bharat Ratna

- Bharat Ratna is India's highest Civilian Award. It was first awarded in 1954.
- The actual award in designed in the shape of a peepal leaf with Bharat Ratna inscribed in Devanagri script in the Sun Figure.
- The reverse side of the decoration Satyameva Jayate has been written in Hindi with an inscription of state emblem.
- The emblem, the Sun and the rim are of platinum. The inscriptions are in burnished bronze.

Winner of Bharat Ratna

- Madan Mohan Malaviya (2015)
- Atal Bihari Vajpayee (2015)
- Sachine Tendulkar (2014)
- CNR Rao (2014)
- Pandit Bhimsen Joshi (2008)
- Lata Dinanath Mangeshkar (2001)
- Ustad Bismillah Khan (2001)
- Prof Amarya Sen (1999)
- Lokpriya Gopinath Bordoloi (1999)
- Loknayk Jayprakash Narayan (1999)
- Pandit Ravi Sanker (1999)
- Chidambaram Subramaniam (1998)
- Madurai Shanmukhavadivu Subbulakshmi (1998)
- Dr Abul Pakir Jainulabdeen Abdul Kalam (1997)
- Aruna Asaf Ali (1997)
- Gulzari Lal Nanda (1997)
- Jehangir Ratanji Dadbhia Tata (1992)
- Maulana Abul Kalam Azad (1992)
- Satyajit Ray (1992)
- Morarji Ranchhodji Desai (1991)
- Rajiv Gandhi (1991)
- Sardar Vallabhai Patel (1991)
- Dr Bhimroa Ramji Ambedakr (1990)
- Dr Nelson Rolihlahla Mandela (1990)
- Marudur Gopalan Ramachandran (1988)
- Khan Abdul Ghaffar Khan (1987)
- Acharya Vinoba Bhave (1983)s
- Kumaraswamny Kamraj (1976)
- Varahagiri Venkata Giri (1975)
- Indira Gandhi (1971)
- Lal Bahadur Shastri (1966)
- Dr Pandurang Vaman Kane (1963)
- Dr Zakir Hussain (1963)
- Dr Rajendraj Prasad (1962)
- Dr Bidhan Chandra Roy (1961)
- Purushottma Das Tandon (1961)
- Dr Dhonde Keshave Karve (1958)
- Pt Govind Ballabh Pant (1957)
- Dr Bhagwan Das (1955)
- Jawaharlal Nehru (1955)
- Dr Mokshagundam Vivesvaraya (1955)
- Chakravarti Rajagoplalchari (1954)
- Dr Chandrasekhara Venkata Raman (1954)
- Dr Sarvapalli Radakrishnan (1954)

Republic Day Awards

Padma Awards

Padma Awards, which were instituted in 1954, is announced every year on the occasion of Republic Day. The award is given in three categories—Padma Vibhushan, Padma Bhushan and Padma Shri. the awards fall in line after the Baharat Ratna.

There are three Padma Awards

- **Padma Vibhushan** is the second highest National Award given for exceptional and distinguished service rendered by government employees.
- **Padma Bhushan** is the third highest National Award given for distinguished service in any field.
- **Padma Shri** is the fourth highest award given for distinguished service in any field.

Gallantry Awards

- **Param Vir Chakra** is the highest decoration of valour awards. It is the most conspicuous act of bravery or some act of valour or self-sacrifice in the presence of the enemy, whether on land, at sea or in the air. The medal is made of bronze.
- **Mahavir Chakra** is the second highest gallantry award for acts of conspicuous gallantry in the presence of the enemy whether on land, at sea or in the air. The medal is made of standard silver.
- **Vir Chakra** is awarded for, acts of gallantry ion the presence of enemy, whether on land, at sea or in the air. The medal is made of standard silver.
- **Ashok Chakra** This is awarded for valour, courageous action or sacrifice, away from the battlefield. It is highest military ward during peacetime.
- **Kirti Chakra** the decoration is awarded for conspicuous gallantry. It is made of standard silver and is circular in shape. The obverse and the reverse are exactly the same as in Ashoka Chakra.
- **Shaurya Chakra** the decoration is awarded for an act of gallantry during peacetime.

Sports Awards

- **Rajiv Gandhi Khel Ratna** is instituted in 1991-92 with the objective of honouring most outstanding sports-person to enhance their general status. It is the highest award bestowed to a sports person in India. The amount of prize money is.

- **Arjuna Award** instituted in 1961 by the Government of India to recognise outstanding achievement in National Sports. The award carries a cash prize of lakh, a bronze statue of Arjuna and a scroll of honour.
- **Dronacharya Award** instituted in 1985 by the Government of India to recognise excellence in sports coaching. The awards carries a cash prize of lakh, a bronze statue of Dronacharya and a scroll of honour.
- **Dhyanchand Award** instituted in 2002, carries a cash prize of lakh, a plaque and a scroll of honour. This honour is given to those sportspersons who have contributed to sportspersons, and sports by their performance and continue to contribute their promotion for sports even after their retirement from active sporting career.

Indian Cinema Awards

Dedasaheb Phalke Award

- Dadasaheb Phalke is known as the Father of Indian Cinema. The highest National Film Award is named after him in 1969.
- This award is given to a film personality for his/her outstanding contribution to the growth and development of Indian cinema. The award comprises of a swarna kamal, a cash prize of and a shawl.
- Dhandiraj Govind (Dadasheb) Phalke's silent feature film, Raja Harishchandra (1913) was first indigenous feature film of India.
- Ardeshir Irani is 1931,j released first full length talkies film Alam Ara.
- Mrs Devika Rani Roerich was the first person to receive Dedasaheb Phlake Award in 1969.

Other National Awards

Bharatiya Jnanpith Awrd

- Instituted in 22nd May, 1961, carries a cash prize of u lakh, a citation and a bronze replica of Vagdevi (Saraswati).
- This award is given for the best literary writing by an Indian citizen in a language listed in Eighth Schedule of the Indian Constitution.

Gandhi Peace Prize

- Established in 2nd October, 1994, on the occasion of the 125th birthday anniversary of Mahantma Gandhi, carries a cash prize of crore.
- Indian Government instituted this annual prize to encourage and promote the significance of Gandhian values over the world.

Indira Gandhi Prize for peace, Disarmament and Development

- Instituted in 1985, this prestigious award io regarded as 'Nobel' and over the years, it has been awarded to those persons who have done outstanding work for international peace, disarmament and development.

Borlaug Award

- Instituted in 1973, carries a cash prize of 5 lakh.
- Instituted to honour outstanding agricultural scientists.

Sahityaj Akademi Award

- Awarded for outstanding literary work and carries a cash prize of 1 lakh.
- Sahitya Academi gives 22 awards for literary works in the languages which has recongnised works.